Kabbalah Glossary
Clarification of terms and concepts of the Kabbalah

Rabbi Raphael Afilalo

From the same author:

The Kabbalah of the Ari Z'al, according to the Ramhal
Kabbalah Editions

Kabbalah Dictionary
Kabbalah Editions

Kabbalists and their works
Kabbalah Editions

160 Questions on the Kabbalah
Kabbalah Editions

Kabbalah concepts 1
Kabbalah Editions

Kabbalah concepts 2
Kabbalah Editions

www.ravraphael.com
www.ramhal.org
www.kabbalah5.com
rav@kabbalah5.com
ravraphael@yahoo.com

Publisher's Cataloging-in-Publication
Afilalo, Raphael
    Kabbalah Glossary: Clarification of terms and concepts
    of the Kabbalah / Raphael Afilalo
    p.cm.
Includes bibliographical references and index.
ISBN 2-923241-07X (Soft cover)
1.Cabala. 2. Mysticism—Judaism. I. Afilalo, Raphael. II.
Title.
BM525. BM723 2005
296.1'6   2005937753

To my mother,
Georgette (Zahra) Afilalo
an exemplary mother
and a woman of valor

MORDECHAI ELIAHU
FORMER CHIEF RABBI OF ISRAEL & RICHON LEZION

מ ר ד כ י   א ל י ה ו
הראשון לציון והרב הראשי לישראל לשעבר

APPROBATION

ב"ה

יהי שם תבס"ד

ראה ראיתי מה שכתב הרב
המפורסם ר' מרדכי שוחט שליט"א
הסכמ רבא ת"א הנה"ח ש"ב
הרמה"ל בישיבה אשר דרכו ותהגן
רבי רבן גמליאל הזן

תקן מעמים ל האמוני ל לעד
בעיר קרת השג כלאים וכל את
דברי הישראל הקדוש הם תולקין
ויסוד ע"י הבן שראל ג' הית ותחת
לביאת כולם לפנת ודבק ה'
בגולה ובקרין ישרא
חתים / הקרם הזיר
מרדכ'

מנחם זאב גרינגלאז

Rabbi M. Z. Greenglass
4987 Plamondon Avenue
Montreal, Quebec
H3W 1E9 Canada (514) 735-6008

Beth Ramhal
JERUSALEM

בס"ד

בית רמח"ל
ירושלים

Jerusalem, Hechvan 7, 5766

To Rabbi Raphael Afilalo

It is important news for the publishing world to propose a dictionary in English on the wisdom of Israel – The Kabbalah.

But let's not forget, that this anthology of words from the highest tradition, gathered in a nomenclature of variable importance, and presented according to the teachings of the Zohar and the Ari Z'al, provides on each word an amount of relative information on its immediate meaning, on its use in the Lurianic Kabbalistic literature and intended for a well defined public. Like a medical dictionary intended for professionals, this work can not be intended for a wide and general audience.

This dictionary on the Kabbalah will be of precious use for serious students already studying the main texts and wishing to further understand the concepts. Of course, only the learning with true masters of this esoteric tradition will allow an enlightenment of what is obscure.

This dictionary will give the reader a just and faithful idea of the authentic Kabbalah, allow him to further expand his knowledge and walk on a clear and concise path.

Rabbi Mordekhai Chriqui
Ramhal Institute
Jerusalem

בס"ד

GRAND RABBINAT DU QUÉBEC

To Rav Raphael Afilalo

September 23, 2005

Dear Raphael,

It is with great interest that I have read your "Kabbalah Dictionary", which brings to the public the explanation of the main concepts and themes of the Lurianic Kabbalah, and the Kabbalah of the Ramhal as well.

It is obvious that your efforts invested in this work, will lead to the results that your explanations and commentaries will be of a great contribution to those who seek to study Kabbalah.

With the blessings of the Torah,

Dr. David Sabbah, Grand Rabbin

RABBI DAVID HANANIA PINTO
Rehov Bayit Vagan 97
Jerusalem · Israël
Tel: (972-2) 643 3605
Fax: (972-2) 641 3945 · 643 3570

דוד חנניה פינטו
רחוב בית וגן 97
ירושלים · ישראל
טל: 026433605
פקס: 026433570 026413945

בס"ד

מוסדות וכוללים ע"ש מרן הצ' מוהר"ח

כ"ק האדמו"ר
רבי חיים פינטו זיע"א
בנשיאות ע"ה
דוד חנניה פינטו
בן הרה"צ כמוהר"ד
רבי משה אהרן
פינטו זיע"א

בע"ה יום חמישי לסד "וישב" תשס"ו

שלום וברכה

המלצה

באתי בזאת להמליץ על הספר *"Kabalah Dictionary"*
(מילון הקבלה) שכתב הרב רפאל אפללו שליט"א. בספר הנ"ל
יש הגדרות ומונחים על קבלת הרמח"ל זיע"א הכל מסדר
בצורה נאה ונוחה ללימוד ולעיון בו.

לאור ההמלצות הרבות שקיבל הספר, נשאר לי רק להמליץ
עליו בכל לב.

אני מברך בזכות אבותי הקדושים זיע"א את המחבר שליט"א
לברכה והצלחה ושיזכה להוציא מתחת ידיו עוד ספרים לזכות
הרבים ושיעלת מעלה בתורה וביראת שמים. אמן

ע"ה דוד חנניה פינטו ס"ט

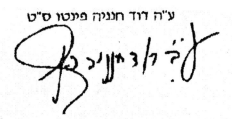

ישיבת נפש חיים
כולל אורות חיים ומשה
כולל משכן בצלאל

רחוב בית וגן 97
ירושלים · ישראל
טל: 02 643 3605
פקס: 02 643 3570 · 02 641 3945

מוסדות אורות חיים ומשה

רחוב האדמו"ר מבלזא 41/7
אשדוד · ישראל
טל: 08 852 1327
פקס: 08 852 4153

OHR HAÏM VÉMOCHÉ

11, Rue Du Plateau
75019 Paris · France
Tel: (33-1) 42 08 25 40
Fax: (33-1) 42 08 50 85

YÉCHIVA PINTO

20 Bis, Rue Des Mûriers
69100 Villeurbanne
France
Tel: (33-4) 78 03 89 14
Fax: (33-4) 78 68 68 45

JERUSALEM · ASHDOD · PARIS · LYON · MONTREAL · TORONTO · BUENOS AIRES · MANCHESTER

בס"ד.

הרבנות הראשית רמלה

לשכת הרב אביחצירא רחוב גולומב 25 רמלה טל. 9225360-08

YEHIEL ABEHSSERA
Grand Rabbin de Ramleh
B.P.4 Ramleh
(ISRAEL)

יחיאל אביחצירא
בלאאמו"ר יצחק אביחצירא זצ"ל
בי"ג להגה"צ מרן אביד יעקב זיע"א
רב העיר רמיים שלישי ט' שבט תשס"בלה

רחוב הרצל 45 ת.ד 4 רמלה טל. בית 9221122-08

שאלות היום

לאלות ישראל אות התשובדרם של הדתנים
האולית שייכו לספרו התשוב ק תל רסולו
10/2015 יבו שילית היואלית ובהתה כפי להויו
ושלם ושוך הקובל? א וין הקטן אבצרם לאוד
והבצלאה דבל אוי יסנה יהסף השת קוזו
אתולוק ישאזור לבבת אות התים לבבת
ו/כאסף

בברכת התורה ולומדיה
יחיאל אבוחצירא
הרב הראשי לרמלה

TIFERES RAMCHAL INSTITUTE
916 EAST 28TH ST.
BROOKLYN, N.Y. 11210
718-692-4055

November 22, 2005

כ חשון תשסו

In the publishing history of books on Kabbalah in the English language there are not many that
can claim to have the potential to truly contribute to the clarification and dissemination of Kabbalah. This sefer by Rabbi Raphael Afilalo is just such a work. It presents in a dictionary format
the range of fundamental concepts that are the bedrock of Kabbalah and which are so crucial for
an individual to master to truly achieve a significant level of proficiency in that area. In that re-
spect in can be said without any reservation at all that this sefer represents a milestone in the publishing of works in Kabbalah in the English language.

Rabbi Raphael Afilalo himself is a true master and teacher of Kabbalah and has actually been
teaching this area of study for many years. In addition, he is a true G-D fearing and righteous Jew,
possessing great knowledge of Torah in general. It is certain that anyone who desires to achieve
a real knowledge of Kabbalah will find this sefer to be of significant assistance toward that endeavor.

I conclude with a blessing that the Almighty should grant success to the dissemination of this sefer
to allow all those who thirst for the knowledge of Kabbalah to acquire it and to also grant its author
health, prosperity, and a long life to enable him to write many more seforim in this all important area.

Sincerely and with all Torah blessings,

Rabbi Mendel Kessin

Rabbi Mendel Kessin
Director , Tiferes Ramchal Institute

DAVID R. BANON

RABBIN DU CENTRE SÉFARADE DE LAVAL
MEMBRE DU BEITH DIN DE MONTRÉAL

דוד רפאל באנון
רב"ד של הקהילה הספרדית בלאוואל
חבר"ד דמונטריאל

יום רביעי פ' האזינו ה'תשנ"ח לעד' אל הדפס של ספרו

לכבוד ידידי הרב רבקה אברהם שליט"א

ראה ראיתי בשמחה את כל תועפת אשר יד ואתה שלחת אל
עניני קבלה בסבא האנשאל ויד כבא צרה אולה או שתה
לכתוב את יסוד הקבלה כדי אותך את רב שתום מנהגן.
וגם הן מבין אותך שתעגנה עוד בהדפס ספרים ובכן הזוי
הן והוחלטה הן יעתוד לך ללב שמחתך.

 שלום ידידך. דוד רפאל באנון

Table of contents

10

Introduction

The goal of this glossary is to provide a genuine clarification of terms and concepts of the true Kabbalah. It is an abridged and simplified version of the Kabbalah Dictionary[1], but the reader will find a clear translation and explanation of the essential terms and concepts, most often encountered in the Kabbalah.

In the very rare books that deal seriously with the subject, the concepts of the Zohar and the Kabbalah are often quoted but not explained. To study Kabbalah, it is important to have a good comprehension of its general idea, as well as its details. It is also necessary to be familiar with its usual terms and appellations, because, particular expressions and metaphors, as well as anthropomorphisms are used. It is of course, well understood, that there is no physical existence at these higher levels. Thus, when terms such as mouth, ears, or other body parts are used, the intention is to describe the esoteric power of these forces, or the position they symbolize.

I have tried to explain the main concepts and expressions used in Hebrew and also in Aramaic. For words or concepts hard to understand out of context, I gave examples of their usage in the Zohar or in the texts of the Ari Z'al or the Ram'hal. I sincerely do hope, that this work will help to clarify these concepts, and be a good contribution towards an understanding of what Kabbalah truly is.
I would like to thank my wife Simona for her patience and encouragements, and my brother Armand, for his friendship and constant support.

---

[1] Kabbalah Dictionary – Rabbi Raphael Afilalo, Kabbalah Editions, 2005

The Kabbalah[2]

The Kabbalah is the mystical and esoteric explanation of the Torah. It teaches the unfolding of the worlds, the various ways of guidance of these worlds, the role of man in the creation, the will of the Creator and so on. No other writings explain in details; the creation of this world and the ones above it, the lights or energies that influence its guidance, nor the final goal of everything. These writings are based on ancient Jewish texts and mostly on the Zohar.

The word Kabbalah comes from the verb *Lekabel* (to receive), but to receive it is first necessary to want, and to become a *Keli* (recipient) able to receive and contain this knowledge.

The Kabbalah teaches us that the world is guided by an extremely complex system of forces or lights, which through their interactions provoke chain reactions that impact directly on man and the worlds. Each one of these reactions has numerous ramifications, with many details and results.

The Kabbalah explains to us the true guidance of the world, so that we may understand the will of G-od. How and why He created the world, in what way He governs it, the provenance of the souls and angels, the purpose of the existence of evil, the reasons for the dualism of reward and punishment, etc.

When one decides that he wants to know his Creator, in learning this science he realizes his smallness compared to these

---

[2] Reproduced from Kabbalah Dictionary – Rabbi Raphael Afilalo, Kabbalah Editions, 2005

incredible forces, the perfection of the Lord and His infinite love
for His creatures.

The Kabbalah also demonstrates to us the importance of man,
because only he, by getting closer to the Creator, can influence
these incredible forces. For this, one has to elevate to a higher
dimension of understanding, and start asking himself some very
important questions like; "Why", "What is the purpose of doing
this act or this prayer", "What are the outcomes of my actions"
etc.

The other writings explain in the least details "how" to do, but
only the Zohar and the Kabbalah explain to us the exact reasons,
and effects of all our prayers and actions.

I believe that most yearn to serve at their best the Creator, but
have been accustomed to execute and not seek further, or were
kept away from this knowledge. It is now the time to know and
learn this magnificent science, as it is written and recommended:

"From there, you shall seek the Lord your G-od, and you
shall find him if you seek him with all your heart, and with
all your soul." (Devarim 4-29)

"The knowledge of the Kabbalah was hidden in those
times and concealed for all these "Talmide 'Hakhamim"
(scholars), except for a few, and even then, discreetly in
small groups and not in public as the Gemarah. But as the
Ari Z'al wrote; especially now for these last generations, it
is allowed and a "Mitsvah" (commandment) to reveal this
science." (Agarot HaKodesh, 26) - Rabbi Sheniur Zalman
Meladi, (Ba'al HaTania)

14

"The one, who was able to learn the secrets of the Torah (Kabbalah) and did not make an effort to understand them, will be severely judged" (Even Shelomoh 85, 24). - HaGra, HaGaon Rabbi Eliyahu de Vilna

"Because of this, the spirit of Moshia'h departs and is not coming for the deliverance... When we are not learning this science (Kabbalah) his coming is delayed." (Commentary of Tikune HaZohar, 81, 92) - HaGra, HaGaon Rabbi Eliyahu de Vilna

"What was decreed from above; not to study the Kabbalah openly, was for a limited time only, until the end of the year 5260. From there, and after it was allowed, and from the year 5300 it was decreed that it is a *"Mitsvah"* (commandment) that old and young should study it. For the merit of studying this and for no other merit, the Moshia'h will come. (Or Ha'Hamah, introduction). -Harav Avraham Azulay (grand-father of the 'Hidah)

All the souls in this present world, that will make the effort to know their Creator through His secret writings (Kabbalah), will ascend higher than all the other souls that did not learn and understand, and will be first at the time of the resurrection. (Zohar, Vayeshev, 182, 2)

The man who learns Kabbalah is above all the others. (Zohar, Shemini, 42, 1)

15

The one that learns Kabbalah to understand the secrets of the Torah, and the purpose of the *Mistvot* according to the *Sod* (secret), is called a "Son" of the Lord. (Zohar, Vayera)

And finally, the very clear obligation in the Torah "To know, now", and not just believe:

"וידעת היום והשבת אל-לבבך כי יהו-ה הוא האלה-ים בשמים ממעל ועל-
הארץ מתחת אין עוד"

"Know, today, and consider it in your heart, that the Lord is G-od in heaven above and upon the earth beneath, and there is no other."

(Devarim. 4-39)

Brief history of the Kabbalah and Kabbalists[3]

First period – The beginning
Aprox. 1750 B.C.E., Erets Israel

Tradition has that one of the first writing of the Kabbalah called "*Sepher HaYetsira*" (The Book of Formation), was composed by Avraham Avinu during this period. It is the first book that mentions a system of ten lights called *Sephirot*.

Second period – The Zohar
Aprox. 240 C.E, Erets Israel

Rabbi Shim'on Bar Yo'hai lived in Galilee in the second century, and was a disciple of Rabbi 'Akiva. To escape the Romans he went into hiding with his son Rabbi El'azar in a cave for thirteen years. During this time, he composed the Zohar which is the esoteric and mystical explanation of the Torah, and the base of most of the Kabbalah writings.

Third Period – Printing of the Zohar
1270, Spain

After having disappeared for about one thousand years, the book of the Zohar is found and printed by Rabbi Moshe de Leon in Spain. This new printing will be disseminated all over Europe, North Africa and the Middle-East and will allow a wider learning of its writings. It is also the period of the "Prophetic Kabbalah" as taught by Rabbi Abraham Abul'afia.

---

[3] [3] Reproduced from Kabbalah Dictionary – Rabbi Raphael Afilalo, Kabbalah Editions, 2005

17

The three Kabbalah schools in Europe
1200 - 1300

In the cities of Provence in France, Gerona in Spain and Worms in Germany were formed three of the main centers of Kabbalah of that period. Under prominent Kabbalists as Rabbi Its'hak the Blind, Rabbi Ezra of Gerona, Rabbi El'azar of Worms, Na'hmanide and others, essential works were published as "*Sepher HaBahir*" "*Sepher Ha'Hesed*" and important commentaries on "*Sepher HaYetsira*".

In France, was developed a type of contemplative mysticism with meditation on the prayers and *Sephirot*. In Spain, an effort was made to bring the major ideas of the Kabbalah to a wider public. In Germany, Rabbi El'azar of Worms had declared that G-od is even closer to the universe and man, than the soul is to the body.

The Tsfat Kabbalists
1500, Tsfat, Israel

After the expulsion from Spain in 1492, some important Spanish Kabbalists as Rabbi Moshe Kordovero, Rabbi Shlomo Alkabetz and Rabbi Yoseph Karo moved to the city of Tsfat in Israel. There, was founded a school of Kabbalah named "New Kabbalah" or "Kabbalah of Tsfat", it is the golden period of the Kabbalah. After this first generation, Rabbi Its'hak Luria Ashkenazi; the Ari Z'al, who was born in Jerusalem, became the leading Kabbalist in Tsfat. He explained and clarified all the main concepts of the Kabbalah, and also innovated in the explanation of the *Sephirot* and *Partsufim (configurations)*. He is the author of the corpus "'*Ets 'Haim*'" which contains all his works in the style of *Sha'are* (entrances), and is today the major reference in Kabbalah.

'Hassidic movement
1700, east Europe

The *'Hassidic* period started with the Ba'al Shem Tov who was the founder of the *'Hassidic* movement. He declared the whole universe, mind and matter to be a manifestation of G-od, and that whoever maintains that this life is worthless is in error, it is worth a great deal; only one must know how to use it properly. The Ba'al Shem Tov's teachings were largely based upon the Kabalistic teachings of the Ari Z'al, but his approach made the benefits of these teachings accessible even to the simplest Jew. Some of the other important leaders that founded their own *'Hassidic* movement are Rabbi Na'hman of Breslev, great grandson of the Baal Shem Tov, Rabbi Shneur Zalman of Liadi, the "*Ba'al HaTanya*", founder of the 'Habad Lubavitch movement.

European masters
1700 -, Europe

At the same time, in other parts of Europe there were other important authorities of the Kabbalah as: Rabbi Moshe 'Haim Luzzatto – Ram'hal who lived in Italy and Amsterdam. From an early age, the Ram'hal had showed an exceptional talent for the study of Kabbalah, it is said that when he was only fourteen, he already knew all the Kabbalah of the Ari Z'al by heart, and nobody knew about it, not even his parents. He was a very prolific writer and wrote on the all aspects of the Torah and the Kabbalah, but because of false accusations, he sadly was persecuted for most of his short life.

Rabbi Eliyahu of Vilna - The Gaon of Vilna who was born in Lithuania. He was one of the main leaders of the *Mitnagdim* (opponents to the *'Hasidic* movement). He is considered to be one of the greatest Torah scholar and Kabbalist of the past two centuries.

Sephardic masters
1700 – North and middle Africa

On the other continent the study of the Kabbalah and mostly the Zohar was also widely spread. Some important scholars are:

Rabbi Shalom Shar'abi - The Rashash who was born in Yemen in 1720, and died in Israel in 1777. When he arrived in Israel, he joined the *Yeshiva* of the *Mekubalim* "*Beth El*" in Jerusalem. He is known as the "Master of the *Kavanot*". His "*Siddur HaRashash*" is the *Siddur* used by some Kabbalists in their everyday prayers, and is based on the *Kavanot* of the Ari Z'al.

Rabbi Ya'acov Abe'htsera who was born in Morocco in 1808, and died in Egypt in 1880. He was a Kabbalist renowned for his piety and for performing miracles. He composed works on all facets of the Torah including important commentaries on the Kabbalistic explanations of the Torah.

Rabbi 'Haim Ben 'Atar – Or Ha'Haim, was born in Morocco in 1696, and died in Israel in 1743. The Ba'al Shem Tov was convinced that the Or Ha'Haim was the Moshia'h of that generation. His main work is the commentary on the Torah; "Or Ha'Haim" where he commented the Torah on the four levels of comprehension, from the *Pshat* (simple), to the Kabbalistic meaning.

Rabbi Yosef 'Haim –The Ben Ish 'Hai, was born in Iraq in 1834, and died in Iraq in 1909. He was a prolific author who wrote at incredible speed. It is known that he would finish writing a complete page before the ink at the top of the page had dried. He explained the *Halakhot* (laws) on the Kabbalistic level but in an accessible language.

The latest Kabbalists
1900 - Israel

Since the beginning of this century, Israel is considered to be the main centre of Kabbalah. One of the most important contemporary Kabbalists was Rabbi Yehudah Ashlag who was born in Poland in 1886, and died in Israel in 1955. His main work is the translation of all the Zohar from Aramaic to Hebrew called "*HaSulam*". Other important Kabbalists are Rabbi Israel Abe'htsera - Baba Sali (1890-1984), Rabbi Yehudah Tzvi Brandwein (1904-1969), Rabbi Avraham Yitzchak HaCohen Kook (1865-1935), Rabbi Yehudah Fatiyah (1859-1942) and others.

Each one of these great Kabbalah scholars brought his own explanations and innovations to this marvelous science. They altogether left a wealth of writings on the Kabbalah which we hope one day, will be more available to the serious learner and seeker of the true Kabbalah.

21

Major concepts in Kabbalah

Hishtalshelut - Chain of events

In the Kabbalah, we learn starting from the first act of G-od in this creation which is the "*Tsimtsum*" (retraction), until the complex arrangements that make the guidance of the worlds. Here, are some of the main concepts of the Kabbalah to better understand this chain of events, and the systems of emanation of the lights and *Sephirot*.

Creation

Tsimtsum - Retraction

In the beginning, there was no existence except His presence, the Creator was alone, occupying all space with His light. His light without end, borders or limit, filled everything. He was not bestowing His influence, because there was no one to receive it. When He willed to create, He started to influence. His light being of such holiness and intensity, it is not possible for any being to exist in its proximity.

The "*Tsimtsum (retraction)*" is the first act of the *Ein Sof* (infinite) in the creation. It is the retraction of His light from a certain space and encircling it, so as to reduce its intensity and allow created beings to exist. After this contraction, a ray of His light entered this empty space, and formed the first *Sephirot*

By these boundaries, He revealed the concepts of rigor and limit needed by the created beings, and gave a space for all the created to exist.

23

'Hallah - Vacant space

It is the space left by the *Tsimtsum* (retraction) of His light. This space is circular and contains all possibilities of existence for separated entities, given that they are distanced from the intensity of His light.

Reshimu - Imprint

When His light retracted forming the round space, a trace of it, called the *Reshimu* (imprint) remained inside the *'Hallal* (vacant space). This lower intensity light, allowed a space of existence (Makom), for all the created worlds and beings.

The roots of all future existence and events are in the *Reshimu* (imprint). Nothing can come into existence, without having its root in this imprint.

Kav - Ray

A straight ray of light called "*Kav*" (ray), emerged from the *Ein Sof* (infinite), and entered on one side of the "'*Hallal*" (vacant space). The combination of the *Kav* (ray) and the *Reshimu* (imprint) is what will give existence to the *Sephirot* with which He governs the worlds.

The *Kav* is the innermost interiority of all this creation.

Sephirot

Sephira

The light of G-od is unique and of equal force and quality. A *Sephira* is in a way a "filter" which transforms this light in a particular force or attribute, by which the *Ein Sof* (Infinite) directs the worlds.

Each *Sephira* is composed of a vessel called *Keli* (recipient), which holds its part of light called *Or* (light). There is no difference in the *Or* (light) itself; the difference comes from the particularity, or position of the *Sephira*. There are ten *Sephirot,* their names are:

Keter	*Crown*	**Tiferet**	*Beauty*
'Hokhma	*Wisdom*	**Netsa'h**	*Glory*
Binah	*Understanding*	**Hod**	*Splendor*
'Hesed	*Bounty*	**Yesod**	*Foundation*
Gevurah	*Rigor*	**Malkhut**	*Kingship*

On the right, the *'Hesed* (kindness*) column: 'Hokhma, 'Hesed, Netsa'h.*
In the middle, the *Ra'hamim* (mercy) *column: Keter, Tiferet, Yesod, Malkhut*
On the left, the *Din* (rigor) column: *Binah, Gevurah, Hod.*

There is one more *Sephira* called *Da'at*, which is counted when *Keter* is not, also in the *Ra'hamim* column. There are also configurations of one or more *Sephirot* acting in coordination, which are called *Partsufim* (configurations).

25

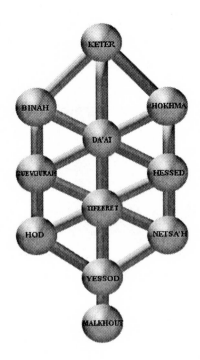

Adam Kadmon - **Primordial man**
World on top of *Atsilut* (emanation)

This first configuration, or the first world where the emanated lights were formed into ten *Sephirot* is called *Adam Kadmon* (Primordial Man). It is the union between the *Reshimu* (imprint) and the *Kav* (ray). From this first configuration, all the other worlds came forth into existence.

Adam Kadmon being at such close proximity to the *Ein Sof* (Infinite), we cannot grasp anything of its nature. Our

26

understanding only starts from the emanations that came out of him in the way of his senses, which are called his branches. From *Adam Kadmon* emerged the four worlds of *Atsilut* (emanation), *Beriah* (creation), *Yetsirah* (formation) and *'Asiah* (action).

Miluyim - Spelling

Letters that are added for the spelling of each individual letter of the Name י-ה-ו-ה

The creative forces or energies are the different powers in the four letters of the name of G-od י-ה-ו-ה, and the various letters added to make their different spellings. Depending on which letters are used, the numerical value of the name changes, and each one of these possibilities becomes different in its nature and actions.

The four *Miluyim* (spellings) are:
- עב, סג , מה, בן - *'A"V* (72), *SaG* (63), *MaH* (45), *BaN* (52)

עב – יוד הי ויו הי   - *'A"V* = 72

סג – יוד הי ואו הי   - *SaG* = 63

מה - יוד הא ואו הא   - *MaH* = 45

בן – יוד הה וו הה   - *BaN* = 52

Each name can also be divided and subdivided as:
'A"V of 'A"V, SaG of 'A"V, MaH of 'A"V ...
BaN of BaN of SaG, SaG of MaH of 'A"V etc.

Shvirat HaKelim - Breaking of the vessels

From the first configuration of *Adam Kadmon* came out different emanations for the construction of the worlds.

From his eyes came out ten *Sephirot* of the aspect of the name of *BaN (52);* they correspond to the feminine aspect - rigor. The three first *Sephirot* of *Keter, 'Hokhma* and *Binah* received and contained their lights, because they were in the three-column arrangement, but the seven lower *Sephirot* were not in the three pillar arrangement needed for the direction of Kindness, rigor and mercy, therefore, they could not hold the influx of their lights and broke. This deficient state caused a fall not only of these *Sephirot*, but of all the worlds also.

This caused an important damage called *Shvirat HaKelim* – the breaking of the vessels; this imperfect arrangement is the first origin of the *Sitra A'hra* or "evil".

Rapa'h Nitsutsot - 288 Sparks

To sustain the *Kelim* (recipients) after they broke, 288 sparks of the lights came down as well, because a connection to their original lights was needed to keep them alive.. The fall of the *Kelim* (recipients), is also called their death.

It is important to understand that all that happens in our world is similar to what occurred in this fall.

The goal of all the works, deeds and prayers of men in this existence, is to help and participate in the ascent of these sparks to their origin. At the completion of this *Tikun* of unification between the fallen sparks and their *Keli* (recipient), it will be the time of the resurrection of the dead and the arrival of *Moshia'h*.

28

Sephirot of MaH (45)

After the breaking of the *Kelim* (recipients) and the separation from their lights, it was necessary for the guidance of the world that reparation be done. From *Adam Kadmon* (Primordial man) came out ten *Sephirot* of the aspect of the name of *MaH (45);* corresponding to the masculine - reparation.

The *Tikun* (rectification) was done by the union of the *Sephirot* of *MaH (45)* (mercy) and *BaN (52)* (rigor) in complex arrangements, as to allow the feminine *BaN* to be repaired by the masculine *MaH,* and for the *Sephirot* to stand in the three-column arrangement of kindness, rigor and mercy.

With the proper order of the *Sephirot* in place, various configurations that are called *Partsufim* completed the creation.

Partsufim – Configurations

Partsuf
A *Partsuf* is a configuration of one or more *Sephirot* acting in coordination.

There are five main *Partsufim* (configurations):
- *Arikh Anpin*
- *Abah*
- *Imah*
- *Zeir Anpin*
- *Nukvah*

And one on top of them: *'Atik Yomin* (clothed inside *Arikh Anpin*).

29

From these five *Partsufim* (configurations); emerge seven more. They emanate as follows:

From *Abah:*
- *Israel Saba* and *Israel Saba* 2
From *Imah:*
- *Tevunah* and *Tevunah* 2
Israel Saba and *Tevunah* are also called by their initials *ISOT* or *ISOT* 2.
From *Zeir Anpin*:
- *Ya'acov* and *Israel*.
From *Nukvah*:
- *Ra'hel* and *Leah*

The *Partsufim Zeir Anpin* and *Nukvah* are the root of all the created. It is by their *Tikunim* (actions) that the guidance of justice is manifested. Here, the "*Tikun*" is a description of the actions, illuminations and inter-relations of the *Sephirot* and *Partsufim*. These *Tikunim* will result in various illuminations of different intensities, for the guidance of the worlds.

Partsuf Zeir Anpin

Zeir Anpin (Z"A) is composed of the six lower *Sephirot*: *'Hesed, Gevurah, Tiferet, Netsa'h, Hod, Yesod* .

The abundance comes down to the world when *Zeir Anpin* and *Nukvah* unite. It is given to *Nukvah,* and from her, to the lower worlds. All this abundance that comes down to the world, proceeds from the various *Zivugim* (unions) of *Z"uN*[4]. Each new day, is of a new emanation that governs it. For each day, there

---

[4] *Zeir Anpin* and *Nukvah*

are new *Zivugim* of different aspects of *Z"uN*. The guidance of the world is dependent on the different positioning and interaction, of *Z"A* and *Nukvah*, since they have a direct effect on the measures and balance of the factors of kindness, rigor and mercy.

The goal of the service of the creatures, is to help prepare the *Partsufim* (configurations) *Z"A* and *Nukvah* for the *Zivug* (union), and this by the elevation and adhesion of the worlds by way of the *Tefilot* (prayers) and *Mitsvot* (commandments).

Partsuf Nukvah

The *Partsuf Nukvah* represents the feminine – the principle of receiving. It comprises of two distinct *Partsufim*: *Ra'hel and Leah*.

The *Partsufim* (configurations) of *Zeir Anpin* and *Nukvah* are the root of all the created. It is by them, that the guidance of justice is manifested. There is perfection for the masculine only when it completes itself with its feminine.

Zivugim - Unions

The *Zivug* is the union of the masculine with its feminine. All the outcomes of the higher emanations are a result of the different unions of the masculine and feminine lights.

There are different kinds of *Zivugim*:
-   the ones for the construction of the worlds
-   for the building of the *Partsufim* (configurations),
-   for the guidance of the worlds.

For the abundance to come down to the world, *Zeir Anpin* needs to unite with *Nukvah*. There can be abundance only when the masculine and the feminine are in harmony. Each day, according to the actions of man, the *Tefilot* during the week, *Shabbat* or holidays, and depending on time, various configurations allow different *Zivugim*, and therefore outflows of abundance of variable intensities.

The guidance of the world is dependent on the different positioning and interaction, of these masculine and feminine *Partsufim*. The results of these unions vary, and produce different emanations of kindness, rigor and mercy.

The goal of the service of the creatures, is to help prepare the *Partsufim* (configurations) *Z"A* and *Nukvah* for the *Zivug* (union), and this, by the elevation and adhesion of the worlds by way of the *Tefilot* and *Mitsvot*.

The four worlds

Atsilut - Emanation
First world

There are four worlds; upon them, the four letters of the Name
ה-ו-ה-י *B'H*, govern.
The first world to unfold from *Adam Kadmon* (Primordial man) is called *Atsilut;* the world of emanation, where there is no existence of the separated, and no *Sitra A'hra* (negative force) even at its lowest levels. It is the first of the four worlds, on top of *Beriah* (creation), *Yetsirah* (formation) and *'Asiah* (action). From *Atsilut* (emanation) unfolded all the lower worlds, which are the

source of existence for the physical worlds, and the possibility of reward, punishment and evil.

Beriah - Creation
World of the souls

The second world is *Beriah* (creation); the world of the *Neshamot*; of the souls.

Yetsirah - Formation
World of the angels

The third world is *Yetsirah* (formation); the world of formation, the world of the angels.

'Asiah - Action
World of physical existence

'Asiah (action) is the fourth world; the world of action, the world of physical existence. The three superior worlds of *Atsilut* (emanation), *Beriah* (creation) and *Yetsirah* (formation), are interior to the fourth world of *'Asiah* (action).

From the last level of the *Sephirot* of *'Asiah* - *Malkhut* of *'Asiah*, the *Sitra A'hra* came out.

Tikunim - Reparation or action

In Hebrew, the word "*Tikun*" has different meanings. It can be understood as reparation or rectification, and also as function, relation or action.

There are different types of *Tikunim:*
- *Tikunim* that took place in the first emanations to repair the worlds
- *Tikunim* for the construction and inter-relations of the *Sephirot* and *Partsufim* (configurations)
- *Tikunim* of certain *Partsufim* (function or action) for the guidance of the worlds
- *Tikunim* (rectifications) for the *Neshamot* (souls).

For the guidance, the *Tikunim* of the *Partsufim* (configurations) are the actions, illuminations and inter-relations of the *Sephirot* and *Partsufim,* and their influence on the worlds. These *Tikunim* result in various illuminations of different intensities, depending on time and the actions of man.

The *Tikun* of the soul is realized by the *Gilgul* (reincarnation), and by the *'Ibur* (attachment).

By giving man a role in the general *Tikun (Tikun 'Olam),* it is now up to him to restore, and make the necessary reparations to the world. However, if man does not act accordingly, the *Tikun* will still be realized, but in the time set by the Creator.

Hanhagua - Guidance

The Kabbalah is the only science that explains to us in the least details, the true guidance of the world, so that we may understand His will. It teaches us that the world is guided by an extremely complex system of forces or lights, which through their interactions provoke chain reactions that impact directly on man and the guidance of the worlds. Each one of these reactions has numerous ramifications with many details and results.

The guidance of the worlds is done through the influence of the different *Sephirot* and *Partsufim* (configurations). It is dependent on the different positioning and interactions of the masculine and feminine *Partsufim*, since they have a direct effect on the measure and balance of the factors of kindness, rigor and mercy. The masculine *Partsufim* bestow kindness, the feminine bestow rigor. By their unions, different equilibriums of the two forces of kindness and rigor make the guidance.

There are two main kinds of guidance:
- The general guidance, which is for the subsistence of the worlds, and is not influenced by the actions of men. This guidance is by the encircling *Sephirot*.

- The variable guidance, which is on the basis of justice, reward and punishment, and is dependant on the actions of men. This guidance is by the linear *Sephirot*.

Ratson Lehashpia' - Will to bestow

The will of the Creator is to bestow goodness on His creatures, all the levels of creation were put in place so His kindness could emanate to them, yet in such a way that they would be able to receive it.

Ratson Lekabel - Desire to receive

By his nature man is himself a *Keli* (recipient) with a will to receive without limits, and containing a spiritual light; his soul. A guidance based on this desire will permit anything without restriction, and not allow man to have merit.

The perfect goal for man is to elevate his bodily desires by sanctifying his ways, and resemble his Creator by becoming a giver with a will to bestow goodness to all.

Giluy Yi'hudo - Revelation of his unity

The goal of all these possibilities of guidance have only one purpose: to allow man to merit by his own efforts, to get closer to his Creator, receive His goodness, and live the *Dvekut* – the adhesion with G-od. In this way, man will attain perfection and be directly involved in the ultimate goal of the creation, which is the revelation of G-od's Sovereignty – *Giluy Ye'hudo.*

Transliteration of the letters

Letter	Name	Equivalent	Transliteration
א	Aleph	A, O, E, I	A, O, E, I
ב	Beit	B, V	B, V
ג	Gimel	G	G
ד	Dalet	D	D
ה	He	H	H
ו	Vav	V	V
ז	Zain	Z	Z
ח	'het		'h
ט	Tet	T	T
י	Yud	Y	Y
כ	Khaf	C, K, KH	C, K, KH
ל	Lamed	L	L
מ	Mem	M	M
נ	Nun	N	N
ס	Samekh	S	S
ע	'ain		'
פ	Pey	P, F	P, F
צ	Tsadey	TS	TS
ק	Kuf	C, K	C, K
ר	Resh	R	R
ש	Shin	S, SH	S, SH
ת	Tav	T	T

GLOSSARY

א"א
A"A
Partsuf Arikh Anpin
Initials

א"ס
E"S
Ein Sof, The without end or limit - Infinite
Initials

א"ק
A"K
Adam Kadmon
Initials

אבא
Abah
Partsuf Abah
One of the five main *Partsufim* (configurations). It is the *Sephira 'Hokhma.*

אבא ואמא
Abah ve Imah
Partsufim Abah and Imah
These two *Partsufim (configurations)* are essential in the guidance of the worlds, they are the link between *Partsuf Arikh Anpin* which is the highest configuration, and *Partsuf Zeir Anpin* who communicates these emanations to the worlds by his *Zivug* (union) with the *Partsuf Nukvah. Abah* is the *Sephira 'Hokhma, Imah* is the *Sephira Binah.*

אבולעפיה
Abul'afia
Rabbi Abraham Abul'afia
Born in 1240 at Saragossa, in Aragon; died in Greece after 1291.
He is the precursor of what is called the "Prophetical Kabbalah" where combinations and permutations of *Autiot* (letters), numerals and *Nikud* (vowels) are symbols which explain and disclose the deepest esoteric meanings. Some of his best known works are: "Sefer ha-Ot" and "Imre Shefer".

אבחנה
Av'hana
Distinction – Insight
Understanding   of   the   deeper   meaning   or   Kabbalistic interpretation.

אביחצירא
Ab'htsera
Rabbi Ya'acov Ab'htsera
Born in Morocco in 1808, died in Dimanhur, Egypt, 1880.
Rabbi Ya'acov was a Kabbalist renowned for his piety and for performing miracles. He composed works on all facets of the Torah including important commentaries on the Kabbalistic explanation of the Torah. Some of his main works are "Makhsof HaLavan", "Pitu'he 'Hotam".

אבי"ע
ABYA
Atsilut, Beriah, Yetsirah and Asiah
Initials of the four worlds.

אבן אבנים
Even Avanim
Stone of stone
Term used for the hardheaded, or the one not willing or ready, to listen and learn.

אבר
Ever
Organ – Limb (Anthropomorphism)
In the language of Kabbalah, anthropomorphisms are used only to illustrate the esoteric power of these forces. It is well understood, that there is no physical existence at these higher levels. Thus, when terms such as mouth, ears, or other body parts are used, the intention is to describe the metaphor, or the position they symbolize.

אברהם
Avraham
Avraham
First patriarch, one of the first books on the Kabbalah "*Sepher HaYetsira*" the "Book of Formation" is attributed to him.
He is represented by the *Sephira 'Hesed.*

אגדה
Agadah
Legend
Also used as a name for Kabbalah.

אדם
Adam
Man – Human
A microcosm of the higher lights and configurations.

אדם הראשון
Adam HaRishon

The First Man

Representation of the *Partsuf* (configuration) *Zeir Anpin* in the book of *Bereshit*.

In the beginning, all the souls were inside *Adam HaRishon*, when he sinned, some fell down to the *Klipot* (negative world) and some remained in him.

אדם קדמון
Adam Kadmon

Primordial man - World on top of Atsilut

This first configuration, or the first world where the emanated lights were formed into ten *Sephirot,* is called *Adam Kadmon* (*Primordial Man*). It is the union between the *Reshimu* (imprint) and the *Kav* (ray). From this first configuration, all the other worlds came forth into existence.

Adam Kadmon being at such close proximity to the *Ein Sof*, we cannot grasp anything of its nature. Our understanding only starts from the emanations that came out of him.

From these emanations, the other four worlds of *Atsilut* (emanation), *Beriah* (creation), *Yetsirah* (formation) and *'Asiah* (action) will unfold.

אדמה
Adamah

Earth

Made from the words Adam (man) and the letter ה (5) as the five levels of the soul.

אדן

Adon

Lord

One of the names of G-od, He is the Lord on all His creation.

אדנ- י

Adona-y

Adona-y

One of the names of G-od, represented by the *Sephira Malkhut*.

אהבה

Ahavah

Ahavah (Love)

Name of a *Hekhal (portal).*

Fifth of seven *Hekhalot,* corresponding to the *Sephira 'Hesed.*

The *Hekhalot* are the different levels of ascension of the *Tefilot* (prayers) before reaching the final seventh *Hekhal* (portal); *Kodesh Hakodashim.*

אהי-ה

AHY-H

One of the names of G-od, represented by the *Sephira Keter.*

או"א

Av"I

Partsufim Abah and Imah

Initials

אוזן חוטם פה

Ozen, 'Hotem, Pey

Ear, nose, mouth

Adam Kadmon being at such close proximity to the Infinite, we

45

cannot grasp anything of its nature. Our understanding only starts from the emanations that came out of him in the way of his senses, which are called his branches. These four branches are called: sight, hearing, smell and speech. They spread out from his eyes, ears, nose, and mouth. in the language of Kabbalah we use names of body parts solely to describe the inner sense, or the position they represent. It is understood, of course, that there is no physical existence at these level.

אוירא

Avirah

Second of the three heads of Partsuf Arikh Anpin

The three heads of *Arikh Anpin* are the roots of the direction of kindness, rigor and mercy. They emanate from *Arikh Anpin* to *Abah* and *Imah,* and from there, to the *Mo'hin* (brains) of *Z"A*.

The second head is *Avirah* - It is in the space between the *Sephirot Keter* and *'Hokhma* of *Partsuf* (configuration) *Arikh Anpin*. Sephira *Da'at* of *Partsuf 'Atik* is clothed Inside it.

אור

Or

Light

Term used to describe an emanation, a force or energy.

אור חוזר

Or 'hozer

Returning light

From the upper realms the lights are emanated to the lower beings in two different ways; with mercy, when they are "facing" toward the receivers and transmitting the light to them in a linear fashion, these are called "linear lights". When the *Sephirot* draw the lights "facing" higher, and transmit the lights by their rear, they are of the aspect of rigor and are called "returning lights".

אור ישר
Or Yashar
Straight, linear light
The *Sephirot* draw the lights from the upper realms to the lower beings with mercy when they are "facing" toward the receivers and transmitting the light to them in a linear fashion, these are linear lights.

אור מקיף
Or Makif
Encircling light
For each *Sephira* and *Partsuf* there are interior and encircling lights.
As for *Z"A*, when his *Mo'hin* are given to him from *Abah* and *Imah* or *ISOT*, they do not enter completely in him; only the *Sephirot NHY* do, the *HGT* and *HBD* stay on top of him, encircling his head.

אור עליון
Or 'Elyon
Upper Light
The original light which left its *Reshimu* (imprint) in the *'Hallal* (vacant space) after the *Tsimtsum* (retraction).
See Reshimu, 'Hallal, Kav, Tsimtsum

אור פנימי
Or Pnimi
Inner Light
The lights that enters and makes the inner light of a *Partsuf* are the *NHY* (Netsa'h, Hod, Yesod) of the superior *Partsuf*.

אורות
Orot
Lights
See Or

אורות האוזן
Orot HaOzen
Lights of the ears
From the ears of *Adam Kadmon* came out ten linear *Sephirot* from the left ear, and ten encircling *Sephirot* from the right ear. They are of the aspect of the name of *SaG* (63).

אורות החוטם
Orot Ha'Hotem
Lights of the Nose
From the nose of *Adam Kadmon* came out ten linear *Sephirot* from the left nostril, and ten encircling *Sephirot* from the right nostril. They are of the aspect of the name of *SaG* (63).

אורות המצח
Orot HaMetsa'h
Lights of the forehead
After the breaking of the *Kelim* (recipients) and the separation from their lights, it was necessary for the guidance of the world that reparation be done. From the forehead of *Adam Kadmon* came out ten *Sephirot* of the aspect of the name of *MaH* (45); corresponding to the masculine - reparation.
The union between the lights of *MaH* (45); which represent mercy, with the ones of *BaN* (52), which represent rigor, made the *Tikun* of the broken *Sephirot*.
See Tikun

אורות העינים

Orot Ha'Enayim

Lights of the eyes

Other lights, of the aspect of the name of *BaN* (52), emerged from the eyes of *Adam Kadmon*. When they came out, they found *Kelim (recipients)* to contain them.

Each one of these *Sephirot* had its own *Keli,* but only the three first ones: *Keter, 'Hokhma* and *Binah,* were structured in the three-column order. However, the seven lower *Sephirot* were aligned one under the other in a straight line, and not ready for the guidance of kindness, rigor and mercy. Therefore, they could not contain their lights and broke. This caused an important damage called *Shvirat HaKelim – the breaking of the vessels.*

See Shvirat HaKelim.

אורות הפה

Orot HaPeh

Lights of the mouth

When the emanations came out from the mouth of *Adam Kadmon,* they did not find an individual *Keli* (recipient) and returned to their origin in the mouth. They did not return completely, only the most tenuous part did, each one leaving its trace. The parts that remained thickened, but were still illuminated by their own parts that ascended.

These lights came out from the same conduit, intermingled, and this is how the concept of *Keli (recipient)* came to be.

אורח תחות חוטמא

Ora'h Ta'hot 'Hotma

Vacant space under the nose

Ora'h Ta'hot 'Hotma is the third of the thirtheen *Tikunim* (action) of the *Dikna* (beard) of *Arikh Anpin,* it corresponds to the vacant

space under the nose.
Each one of these *Tikunim* has its particular function or action for
the general guidance.

אורח תחות פומא
Orot Ta'hot Puma
Space under the mouth
Orot Ta'hot Puma is the fifth of the thirtheen *Tikunim* (action) of
the *Dikna* (beard) of *Arikh Anpin,* it corresponds to the space
under the mouth
Each one of these *Tikunim* has its particular function or action for
the general guidance.

אוריתא
Auraita
Torah
The Kabbalah is the mystical and esoteric explanation of the
Torah.
The Torah contains four levels of comprehension, of which the
highest is the *Sod (secret)*. At this level, we understand that our
Tefilot and the accomplishment of each one of the *Mitsvot* has a
direct influence on the superior worlds and on their guidance. Only
man, by praying and the accomplishment of the *Mitsvot* can
influence these incredible forces. As there are 613 veins and
bones to man, similarly, there are 613 parts to the soul and 613
Mitsvot in the Torah, this number is not arbitrary as there are
important interrelations and interactions between them.

אות
Ot
Sign
Alliance as the *Brit* (circumcision), *Tefilin* etc.

אותיות

Autiot

Letters

The *Autiot* are the expression of the *Ma'hshava* (thought). In combination with the *Ta'amim (cantillation)*, *Nekudot* (vowels), *Tagin* (crowns), or with other letters, they transform the higher lights into action. There are twenty two letters and five ending letters. The five ending letters correspond to the *Gevurot* (rigors).

The creative forces or energies are the different powers in the four letters of the name of G-od י-ה-ו-ה, and the various letters added to make their different spellings.

All the emanations are in the order of this name and all the configurations are drawn from these four letters and their different spellings, which are called *Miluyim* (spelling of the letters). Depending on the *Miluyim* of these letters, we obtain different names as: *'A"V* (72), *SaG* (63), *MaH* (45) and *BaN* (52).

Each name can also be subdivided, as: *'A"V* of *'A"V*, *SaG* of *"A"V*, *MaH* of *'A"V* ...*BaN* of *BaN* etc. When these names act in combination with each other, more interrelations and different actions occur. The *Autiot* correspond to the name of *BaN* (52), and to the world of *Asiah*.

אחד

E'had

One – Unique

One of the qualities of the Creator.

Until the world was created, He and His Name were one.

The light of G-od is unique, of equal force, quality and beyond all description. Since the concept of limitlessness is above our human comprehension, we therefore have to use terms accessible to our understanding. In the Kabbalah, the term 'quality' is used, to differentiate the various transformations of this "unique light", and to help us understand its effects upon the guidance of the worlds.

The *Sephirot* or *Partsufim* are called the attributes or qualities of G-od. A *Sephira* is in a way a "filter" which transforms this unique light in a particular force or quality, by which the Creator guides the worlds.

See Sephirot, Partsufim

אחור

A'hor

Backside – Behind

In general it represents rigor.

אחור באחור

A'hor Be A'hor

Back to Back

There is a notion of closeness and interaction, depending on whether the *Partsufim* (configurations) face or turn their back to each other. The three possibilities are: face to face, face to back, or back to back.

Back to back is the lowest level, and corresponds to dissimulation and rigor.

אחור בפנים

A'hor B Panim

Back to Face

There is a notion of closeness and interaction, depending on whether the *Partsufim* face or turn their back to each other. The three possibilities are: face to face, back to face, or back to back.

Back to face is the second level, between the face to face which is the ideal level and corresponds to the bestowing of abundance, and back to back which corresponds to dissimulation and rigor. Back to face denotes a readiness to get close from one side only. It is a position of waiting or longing for the ideal face to face situation.

אחוריים

A'horaim

Rears

Sephirot Netsa'h, Hod and *Yesod (NHY)* of a *Sephira* or *Partsuf.* The *Klipot* (husks) can only attach to the *rears (NHY)* of the *Sephirot* or *Partsufim.*

אחיזה

A'hizah

To hold – Attach

The *Klipot* (husks) nourish themselves by attaching to the exteriority of the *Sephirot.* They get their livelihood from the higher lights and gain more power to act negatively. These negative forces can only get strength when men sin, and are not doing G-od's will.

See Sitra A'hra

אחר

A'her

Other

Name also used for the other side or negative force.

אילן

Ilan

Tree

The disposition of the *Sephirot* in the three pillars arrangement is called the *Sephirotic* tree.

אילנה דחיי
Ilana De'Haye
Tree of life
See *'Ets Ha'Haim*

אילנה דמותא
Ilana de Motah
Tree of Death
During the night the "Tree of Life" ascends higher and the "Tree of death" governs. It is only in the morning that the governance is given back to the Tree of Life and that all the souls return in men's bodies. (Zohar, Bamidbar)

אין סוף
Ein Sof
The without end or limit - Infinite
One of the names of G-od.
The Name of G-od that is the most used in the Kabbalah.
His light is perfect, and cannot be measured by any definition or limiting terms. If we think about definitions, we introduce a notion of limit, or absence of its opposite. Being ourselves distinct separate beings, we cannot grasp the concept of the "non-distinct". Everything we know is finite, by having a measure or an opposite. We therefore use the name "*Ein Sof*" (without limit) since we know and admit that G-od and the concept of limitlessness or without end is beyond our human comprehension.

אל
El
One of the names of G-od, represented by the *Sephiran 'Hesed.*

אל חי

El 'Hay

One of the names of G-od, represented by the *Sephira Yesod*.

אלוה-ים

Elohi-m

One of the names of G-od, represented by the *Sephira Gevurah*. In general it denotes rigor in the actions of G-od.

אלוה-ים צבאות

Elohi-m Tsebaot

One of the names of G-od, represented by the *Sephira Hod*.

אלכסון

Alakhson

Diagonal

There are lights or *Partsufim* (configurations) that are diagonal to a more important *Partsuf*.

In diagonal on the two sides of *Partsuf Z"A*: "*The Clouds of Glory*" on his right, and "*The Manna*" on his left.

In diagonal on the two sides of *Partsuf Leah D'hM*: "*The Scepter of Elokim*", and "*The Scepter of Moshe*".

In diagonal on the two sides of *Partsuf Ya'acov*: "'*Erev Rav*" on his right, and "'*Essav*" on his left.

These other lights, or *Partsufim* are not considered as complete *Partsufim*; their actions are temporary and at particular times only.

אמא

Imah

Partsuf Imah

One of the five main configurations. It is the *Sephira Binah*. She dresses the left arm (*Gevurah*) of *Partsuf Arikh Anpin*. Her three

55

lower *Sephirot (NHY (Netsa'h, Hod, Yesod))* dress on the *NHY* of *Partsuf Abah, together they* make the *Mo'hin (brains)* of *Partsuf Z"A.* Her *Zivug (union)* with *Partsuf Abah* is constant.

See Abah ve Imah

אמצע
Emtsa'h
Middle
Some *Sephirot* as *'Hesed, Gevurah, Tiferet, Netsa'h and Hod* have three parts: first, middle and third. These parts emanate their lights or actions independently.

אספקלריא דלא נהרא
Aspaklaria de lo Nehara
Non luminous mirror
From *Adam Kadmon,* different emanations spread out as a preparation for the future worlds. One of these first emanations came out from its mouth; these lights did not find an individual *Keli* (recipient) and returned to their origin in the mouth. They did not return completely, only the most tenuous part did, each one leaving its trace. The parts that remained thickened, but were still illuminated by their own parts that ascended.

When the light of the *Sephira Keter* went back up, it did not come out again, *Sephira 'Hokhma* came out and took its place, *Sephira Binah* took the place of *'Hokhma,* and so on, until *Sephira Malkhut* was left with no light, like a "non luminous mirror."

אצילות
Atsilut
World of Emanation
From the first configuration; *Adam Kadmon,* four worlds unfolded.

The first world to unfold is called *Atsilut*; the world of emanation, where there is no existence of the separated and no *Sitra A'hra* (evil), even at its lowest levels. It is the highest of the four worlds, on top of the worlds of *Beriah*, *Yetsirah* and *'Asiah*.

It consists of five main *Partsufim* (configurations): *Arikh Anpin*, *Abah*, *Imah*, *Zeir Anpin* and *Nukvah*.

From *Atsilut* unfolded all the lower worlds, which are the source of existence for the physical worlds, the possibility of reward, punishment and evil.

At the bottom of *Atsilut* lights collided, and a curtain was made between *Atsilut* and *Beriah* from the striking of these lights. From there, other *Partsufim* similar to the ones in *Atsilut* were formed in the lower worlds, but of a lower force since the lights were dimmed by the curtain. It is because of the diminution of these light's intensities, that existence for separated entities became possible.

אצילות בריאה יצירה עשייה
Atsilut, Beriah, Yetsirah and 'Asiah

From the first configuration; *Adam Kadmon* (*Primordial man*) emanations made the four lower worlds. There is a screen (divider) that separates one world from another, and from this screen the ten *Sephirot* of the lower world came out from the ten *Sephirot* of the higher world.

The first world is *Atsilut* — the world of emanation. Under the divider of *Atsilut* is the world of *Beriah* (creation) - the world of the *Neshamot* (souls). Under the divider of *Beriah* is the world of *Yetsirah* (formation) - the world of the angels. Under the divider of *Yetsirah* is the world of *'Asiah* (action) - the physical world.

Atsilut is of the aspect of *Partsuf Abah* (configuration), *Beriah* of *Imah*, *Yetsirah* of *Z"A,* and *'Asiah* of *Nukvah*.

All the worlds are similar (they all contain 10 *Sephirot* and five *Partsufim*), but the quintessence of the higher is superior.

See Atsilut, Beriah, Yetsirah, Asiah

אר"י

Ari

See Ari Z'al

ארוך

Arokh

Long

Some *Sephirot* are longer and reach higher or lower than others.

ארי ז"ל

Ari Z'al

Rabbi Its'hak Luria Ashkenazi

Born in Jerusalem in 1534, died in 1572 in Tsfat, Israel.

He was the leading Kabbalist in Tsfat; he explained and clarified all the main concepts of the Kabbalah. He also innovated in the explanation of the Sephirot and Partsufim (configurations). He is the author of the corpus "Kitve HaAri" which contains all his works in the style of Sha'are (entrances). His main work is the "Ets 'Haim".

אריך אנפין

Arikh Anpin

Partsuf – Long countenance

It is the main *Partsuf* (configuration) in each world. All the other *Partsufim* are his "branches". He is called *Arikh Anpin* and his *Nukvah* (feminine), together they make one *Partsuf;* the masculine on the right and the feminine on the left.

Arikh Anpin reaches from the top to the bottom of *a world, Abah* and *Imah* dress his right and left arm,

The emanations and actions of *Partsuf Arikh Anpin* are called his *Tikunim,* its three heads are the roots of the direction of kindness, rigor and mercy.

See Tikunim, Partsuf

אש
Esh

Fire

One of the four main levels of *Klipot* (negative husks) corresponding to the four lower worlds is called *"Eish Mitlaka'hat"* - *A dividing fire.*

אשלג
Ashlag

Rabbi Yehudah Ashlag

Born in Poland 1886, died in Israel in 1955.

One of the main contemporary Kabbalists. His main work is the translation of all the Zohar from Aramaic to Hebrew called "HaSulam" and "Talmud 'Eser HaSephirot".

אשת-חיל עטרת בעלה
Eshet Hail Ateret Ba'la

A virtuous woman is a crown of her husband

There can be abundance only when the masculine and the feminine are in harmony.

For the abundance to come down to the world, *Partsuf Zeir Anpin* needs to unite with *Partsuf Nukvah*. He has to build her and wait until she comes from the back to back to the front-to-front position for the *Zivug* (union).

אתב"ש
ATBaSH

Permutation of letters to understand hidden meanings of words.
First letter replaced by the last, second by the before last etc.

ב"ן

BaN *(52)*

Miluy (spelling) of the name י-ה-ו-ה with a total of 52

The creative forces or energies are the different powers in the four letters of the name of G-od י-ה-ו-ה, and the various letters added to make their different spellings. Depending on which letters are used, the numerical value of the name changes, and each one of these possibilities becomes different in its nature and actions.

The four *Miluyim* (spellings) are:

עב ,סג , מה, בן - *'A"V, SaG, MaH, BaN* -

-

יוד הי ויו הי – עב   - *'A"V* = 72

יוד הי ואו הי – סג   - *SaG* = 63

יוד הא ואו הא - מה   - *MaH* = 45

יוד הה וו הה – בן   - *BaN* = 52

Each name can also be divided and subdivided as:

'A"V of 'A"V, SaG of 'A"V, MaH of 'A"V ...

BaN of BaN of SaG, SaG of MaH of 'A"V etc.

The name *BaN* (52) is the *Miluy* (spelling) of the name י-ה-ו-ה with the letter ה

יוד הה וו הה – בן   - *BaN* = 52

It corresponds to the feminine aspect - rigor, and is the root of deterioration. When it came out through the eyes of *Adam Kadmon*, its three first *Sephirot* – KHB (Keter, 'Hokhma, Binah) were able to stand in three columns, the seven lower *Sephirot* could not stand in this order and broke.

The *Tikun* (rectification) is the union of the *Sephirot* of MaH *(45)*

(mercy) and *BaN (52)* (rigor) in complex arrangements, as to allow the feminine *BaN (52)* to be repaired by the masculine *MaH (45)*, and for the *Sephirot* to stand in the three-column arrangement of kindness, rigor and mercy
See Orot Ha'Enayim, Sephirot Shel BaN

בוהו
Bohu
Void
The world of *Shvirat HaKelim* (breaking of the vessels).

בוצינא
Butsina
Light
See Or

בוצינא קדישא
Butsina Kadisha
The saintly light or lamp
Name given to Rabbi Shim'on Bar Yo'hai, author of the Zohar.

בורא
Boreh
The Creator
One of the names of G-od.

בחינה
Be'hinah
Aspect - Feature – Quality
The light of G-od is unique, of equal force, quality and beyond all description. Since the concept of limitlessness is above our

human comprehension, we therefore have to use terms accessible to our understanding. In Kabbalah the term 'quality' is used, to differentiate the various transformations of this "unique light", and to help us understand its effects upon the guidance of the worlds.

The *Sephirot* or *Partsufim* are called the attributes or qualities of G-od. A *Sephira* is in a way a "filter" which transforms this light in a particular force or quality, by which the Creator guides the worlds.

See Sephirot, Partsufim

בחירה

Be'hirah

Choice

Since the intention of the Creator is to bestow goodness on His creatures, all the levels of creation were put in place so His kindness could emanate to them, yet in such a way that they would be able to receive it. Complete rigor will be the destruction of anything not perfect, while complete kindness will permit everything without restriction. However, these two aspects are necessary to make the guidance of kindness and justice and to give man the possibility of serving the Creator by their free will.

After the *Shvirat HaKelim* (breaking of the vessels) with the emanation of the lights of the name *MaH (45)* and *BaN (52)*, He could have done the *Tikun* (repair) of all the worlds, but then, there would not have been a reason for the participation of man in this *Tikun*. For man to have a possibility to act and repair the creation, G-od restrained in a way, his outflow of kindness to this world, to give men the merit of doing the *Tikun* with their free will. The root of the *Sitra A'hra* (negative force) is in the lack, or absence of the *Kedushah* (holiness). Its existence was willed by the Creator to give man free choice.

The good deeds of man have an effect on the four higher worlds, his bad deeds; on the four lower worlds. It is only when man sins, that the negative side can grow in strength. His negative aspect (his *Yetser Hara'*) grows inside him, cuts him off from the higher worlds, and uproots him from the *Kedushah*. I
The two aspects of *Yetser Tov* and *Yetser Hara'* are also necessary for the guidance of justice, and to give man the possibility of free choice.

ביאור
Biur
Explanation
Clarifications and explanations are needed to understand the sometimes complex concepts of the Kabbalah.

ביטול
Bitul
Nullification
There is sometimes nullification of an inferior force or emanation, when a higher one intervenes.

בינה
Binah
Sephira (understanding)
Third of the *Sephirot*.
Quality: Kindness to all, even to the less deserving (but from her, the rigors start).
Column: Left – *Din* (rigor)
Position: Top – left

Other *Sephirot* on the same column: *Gevurah, Hod.*

Partsufim made from this *Sephira:*

- *Imah*

- From *Malkhut* of *Binah -Tevunah*

- From Malkhut of Tevunah - Tevunah 2

Corresponding name: *YHV-H*   י-ה-ו-ה *(but with the vowels of Elokim)*

Corresponding *Miluy* (spelling) of name: *SaG (63)* - סג

Corresponding vowel: *Tsere*

Physical correspondence: Left brain

Level of the soul: *Neshama*

See Sephira, Partsuf

 בירור

Birur

Selection or clarification

Act of separation between the positive and negative.

בית המקדש

Beit ha

Mikdash

The Temple

When the Temple was built, the guidance of *'Hesed* – Kindness was prevailing.

בעל שם טוב

Ba'al Shem Tov

Rabbi Israel Ben Eliezer

Born in 1698 in Russia, died in Ukraine in 1760

The founder of the 'Hassidic movement. He declared the whole universe, mind and matter, to be a manifestation of G-od, and that whoever maintains that this life is worthless is in error, it is worth a great deal; only one must know how to use it properly. Being a living legend, the Ba'al Shem Tov spent most of his time in worship, serving G-od, teaching his disciples, and giving blessings to the thousands that came to see him.

One of his favorite sayings was that no man has sunk too low to be able to raise himself to God.

בקיעה

Beki'ah

Cleaving

Emanations or lights can cleave out from an inside to the outside.

ברוך הוא

Barukh Hu

Blessed He is

Used after the pronunciation or writing of G-od's names.

בריאה

Beriah

World of creation – of the souls

From the first configuration of *Adam Kadmon,* four worlds unfolded.

On these four worlds, the four letters of the Name (י-ה-ו-ה) *B'H,* govern.

י in *Atsilut;* by it, all the repaired levels are put in order.

ה descends from it (*Atsilut*) to *Beriah,* and guides it.

ו to *Yetsirah,* and ה to *'Asiah.*

The second world to unfold is called *Beriah*; the world of creation. It is the world of the *Neshamot* (souls). It is under *Atsilut* and on top of *Yetsirah* and *'Asiah.*

At the bottom of *Beriah,* the lights of its *Malkhut* collided, and a curtain was made between *Beriah* and *Yetsirah* from the striking of these lights. From there, other *Partsufim* similar to the ones in *Beriah* were formed in the lower worlds, but of a lower force since the lights were dimmed by the curtain. It is because of the diminution of these light's intensities, that existence became possible for even more separated entities as angels and man.

In parallel to the four worlds (*ABYA*), there are four types of existence in our world; mineral corresponding to *'Asiah (action),* vegetal corresponding to *Yetsirah (formation),* animal corresponding to *Beriah (creation),* and man corresponding to *Atsilut (emanation).*

The world of *Beriah (creation)* is of the aspect of *SaG (63).* Thus, *Beriah* is of the aspect of *Partsuf Imah – Sephira Binah.*

בר יוחאי

Bar Yo'hay

Rabbi Shim'on Bar Yo'hay

Born in Galilee and died in Meron, Israel during the 2nd century.

He was a disciple of Rabbi Akiva. To escape the Romans he went into hiding with his son Rabbi El'azar in a cave for thirteen years. During this time he composed the Zohar which is the esoteric and mystical explanation of the Torah, and the base for most of the Kabbalah writings.

ברייה

Briah

Creature

Of the four worlds, three contain separate creatures. *Neshamot* (souls) in *Beriah* (creation), angels in *Yetsirah* (formation), physical beings in *'Asiah* (action).

ברית
Brit
Covenant – Circumcision
Represented by the *Sephira Yesod*.

ברכה
Berakhah
Blessing
When saying the blessing with the Kabbalistic meditation on the appropriate words or names, we act and participate directly on the *Tikun* (repair) of the thing being blessed.
See Kavanot

ברסלב
Breslev
Rabbi Na'hman of Breslev
Born in Russia in 1772, died in Uman, Russia in 1811
Rabbi Na'hman was the great grandson of the Ba'al Shem Tov. He gave great importance to "Dvekut" (attachment to G-od) and pure joy. Some of his main works are "Likutey Moharan", "Tikun HaKlali" and his well known stories and fables.

ג' ראשונות

Shalosh Rishonot

The three first Sephirot

Keter, 'Hokhma, Binah

The roots of all the created are in the seven lower *Sephirot*, the three first *Sephirot* are like a crown on them to repair and direct them. In the three first *Sephirot* there is not really a notion of damage, they are above men's deeds, and are not affected by their sins.

ג"ר

G"aR

The three first Sephirot

Keter, 'Hokhma, Binah

גבול

Gevul

Boundary – Limit

By putting boundaries to His light, the Creator revealed the concepts of rigor and limit needed by the created beings, and gave a space for all the created to exist.

See Tsimtsum

גבורה

Gevurah

Rigor

The light of G-od is unique, of equal force, quality and beyond all description. In Kabbalah the term 'quality' is used, to differentiate the various transformations of this "unique light", and to help us understand its effects upon the guidance of the worlds.

The *Sephirot* or *Partsufim* (configurations) are called the attributes or qualities of G-od. A *Sephira* is in a way a "filter" which transforms this light in a particular force or quality, by which the Creator guides the worlds. One of these manifestations of this light once filtered by the *Sephira Gevurah* emanates rigor.

The *Sephirot* are arranged in three columns: right, left and middle, representing the guidance of the world in the manner of *'Hesed*, *Din* and *Ra'hamim* - Kindness, rigor and mercy. In the attribute of rigor, the guidance is from the left pillar – the pillar of rigor, it contains the *Sephirot*: *Binah*, *Gevurah*, *Hod*. The corresponding name to this attribute is: *Elohi-m* - אלהי-ם

Some *Partsufim* are masculine and bestow kindness, others are feminine and bestow rigor. By their union, different equilibriums of these two forces (Kindness and rigor), make the guidance. Complete rigor will be the destruction of anything not perfect, while complete kindness will permit everything without restriction. Thus we see that everything that is, and happens, is always composed of a variable measure and balance of these two forces.

Rigor is mostly manifested by all the feminine aspects as: the name of *BaN (52)*, the *Sephira Gevurah* and by all the concealments of the masculine aspects which represent bounty.

There are particular moments, or days of rigor during the year, this is dependent on the different position of the *Partsufim*. In the absence of *Zivug* (union) between these *Partsufim* when the masculine and feminine *Partsuf* are back to back, it corresponds to dissimulation and rigor.

גבורה

Gevurah

Sephira (Rigor)

Fifth of the *Sephirot*.

Quality: Full rigor to who is deserving.

Column: Left – *Din* (rigor)
Position: Left – Middle
Other *Sephirot* on the same column: *Binah, Hod.*

Partsufim made from this *Sephira:*
One of the *Sephirot* that make the *Partsuf Z"A.*
Corresponding name: *Elohi-m* אלהי-ם
Corresponding *Miluy* (spelling) of name: *MaH* (מה) 45
Corresponding vowel: *Sheva*
Physical correspondence: Left arm
Level of the soul: *Rua'h*
See Gevurah, Sephira, Partsuf

גבורות
Gevurot
Rigors
For the guidance, five emanations of the aspect of *'Hesed* (kindness) and five emanations of the aspect of *Gevurah* (rigors), are given by the *Sephira Da'at* to the *Partsufim* (configurations) *Z"A* and *Nukvah*. *Partsuf Z"A* receives the five *'Hasadim* and *Nukvah* receives the five *Gevurot*.
Rigor is also manifested by the five ending letters: מנצפך, they are called the five *Gevurot.*
See Gevurah, Mayin Nukvin

גדול
Gadol
Big – Adult
A *Partsuf* (configuration) is called big or adult when it has received all his *Mo'hin* (brains), and is in *Gadlut* (growth) 1 or *Gadlut* 2.
See Gadlut, Zeir Anpin

71

גדלות
Gadlut
Adulthood – Growth
The *Gadlut* of a *Partsuf* (configuration) is its final stage of growth, when it is able to act with all its strength. There are two stages of *Gadlut*: *Gadlut* 1 and *Gadlut* 2.

At first, *Z"A* goes through a period of gestation, followed by a first period of infancy and a first growth. Afterwards, there is a second period of infancy and growth. It is only after the second growth that a *Partsuf* is considered fully grown.

See Mo'hin, Partsuf, Z"A

גדלות ראשון של ז"א
Gadlut rishon shel Z"A
First growth of Z"A
The *Gadlut* of a *Partsuf* (configuration) is its final stage of growth, when it is able to act with all its strength. At first, *Partsuf Z"A* is in a state of *Dormita* (somnolence), to act it needs to get his *Mo'hin* (brains) from *Partsuf ISOT* or *Partsuf Abah* and *Imah*, and to get to a stage of growth.

Inside of *Partsuf Imah*, *Z"A* goes through a period of gestation, followed by a first period of infancy and a first growth. In the first growth his *Mo'hin* are from *NHY* (Netsa'h, Hod, Yesod) of *Partsuf Tevunah*. During the time of the gestation, *Z"A* is not really acting as it is being built, at the time of suckling it starts to act, and at the growth it is ready to act. This is *Gadlut* 1.

גדלות שני של ז"א
Gadlut sheni shel Z"A
Second growth of Z"A
The *Gadlut* of a *Partsuf* (configuration) is its final stage of growth, when it is able to act with all its strength. After its first growth, *Z"A*

goes through a second period of gestation, followed by a second period of infancy and a second of growth. In the second growth, his *Mo'hin* are directly from *Abah* and *Imah* and enter in the same way as in the first growth.

It is only after the second growth, that *Z"A* has reached its full potential. This is *Gadlut* 2.

גוף

Guf

Body

A *Partsuf or Sephira* has two parts; its head which are the three first *Sephirot* of *Keter, 'Hokhma, Binah,* and its body which are the seven other *Sephirot.*

See Sephira, Partsuf

גזרה

Gezera

Decree – Edict

One of the important decrees, and for reasons only known to Him, the Creator decreed that man should not be able to see the truth and the finality of everything without much effort.

גידים

Gidim

Sinews

There are 613 parts to the soul, similarly, there are 613 *Mitsvot*, and 613 sinews and bones to man, this number is not arbitrary, as there are important interrelations and interactions between them.

גילוי

Giluy

Revelation – Clarity

There are periods of more or less revelation, depending on time and the positions of the *Partsufim (configurations)*.

גילוי יחודו

Giluy Yi'hudo

Revelation of his unity

The goal of all the complex inter-relations and possibilities of guidance have only one purpose: to allow man to merit by his own efforts, to get closer to his Creator, and live the *Dvekut* – the adhesion with G-od. In this way, man will attain perfection and be directly involved in the ultimate goal of the creation, which is the revelation of G-od's sovereignty *–Giluy Ye'hudo*

גימטריה

Gematria

Numerical values of the letters

Each letter has its own numerical value. The fact that some words have the same numerical value is not just coincidence, but denotes a similarity or complementarity.

There are seven main types of *Gematriot*:

Ragil, Katan, HaKlali, Kolel, HaKadmi, HaPerati, Miluy

1 - *Ragil*: the numbers of the letters are as follows:

From	To	Value
א	ט	1 - 9
י	צ	10 -90
ק	ת	100 - 400
ך	ץ	500 -900

Ex :   הארץ = 1106

2 – *Katan*: tens and hundreds are reduced to one digit.

From	To	Value
א	ט	1 - 9
י	צ	1 - 9
ק	ת	1 - 4
ך	ץ	5 -9

Ex : הארץ = 17

3 – *HaKlali*: the *Ragil* value of the word squared.
Ex : הארץ = 1106 * 1106 = 1 223 236
4 – *Kolel*: the *Ragil* value of the word + the numbers of letters, or + 1 for the word.
Ex : הארץ = 1106 + 4 = 1110 or 1106 + 1 = 1107
5 – *HaKadmi* : each letter has its *Ragil* value plus the total of all the ones preceding it.

From	To	Value
א	ט	1 - 45
י	צ	55 – 495
ק	ת	595 –1495
ך	ץ	1995 – 4995

Ex : הארץ = 15+1+795+4995 = 5806

6 – *HaPerati* : each letter is squared.
Ex : הארץ = 5 * 5 = 25, 1 * 1 = 1
200 * 200 = 40 000, 900 * 900 = 810 000 Total = 850 026
7 – *Miluy:* the sum of the spelling of each letter.

Letter	Miluy	Value
ה	הא	6
א	אלף	111
ר	ריש	510
ץ	צדי	104

Ex : הארץ = 731

See Miluy

גימל בגימל
Gimel Be Gimel
Three on three

After the *Shvirat HaKelim* (breaking of the vessels), when the lights were separated from their recipients, the first act of reparation for this damage was to reunite again these fallen lights and recipients.

Partsuf Arikh brought up his three lower *Sephirot – Netsa'h, Hod, Yesod* on to clothe his three higher *Sephirot - 'Hesed, Gevurah, Tiferet*, three *(NHY)* on three *(HGT)*.

This was the first force given to the broken recipients of the seven *Sephirot* to ascend to their lights.

גלגול
Gilgul
Reincarnation

The soul has five names: *Nefesh, Rua'h, Neshama, 'Hayah* and *Ye'hidah*, which correspond to its five levels. The soul is the spiritual entity inside the body, the latter being only his outer garment.

Each level of the soul is subdivided in five levels. As for the level of *Nefesh;* there are *Nefesh* of *Nefesh, Rua'h* of *Nefesh, Neshama* of *Nefesh, 'Hayah* of *Nefesh* and *Ye'hidah* of *Nefesh.*

As there are for each of the five worlds; ten *Sephirot* and five *Partsufim* (configurations). Each soul has its origin corresponding to one of these levels. Therefore, a soul could be from the level of *Nefesh* of *Malkhut* of *Nukvah* of *'Asiah,* or *Rua'h* of *'Hesed* of *Abah* of *'Yetsirah,* or *Neshama* of *Abah* of *Z"A* of *Yetsirah* etc.

The higher levels of the soul cannot be acquired at once. Most men only have the level of *Nefesh,* and if they merit, they will acquire the next levels - but one by one.

To reach the next higher level of his soul, man must do the *Tikun* (rectification) of the preceding level. The *Tikun* of the soul is realized by the *Gilgul* (reincarnation), and by the *'Ibur* (attachment). The *Gilgul* is the reincarnation of a soul from the time of birth until death, the *'Ibur* is an attachment of another soul to his, which could come and leave anytime.

By accomplishing what he did not accomplish of the 613 *Mitsvot* (commandments), man makes the necessary *Tikun* of his soul, which can now elevate to the higher realms and rejoin its source. But if man does not do the *Tikun* of the level of his soul for which he came, he comes back and reincarnates.

For the *Mitsvot* that it was obligated to accomplish, it accomplishes them by the *Gilgul*, for the ones it did not have to accomplish, it accomplishes them by the *'Ibur,* which departs afterwards.

To help him accomplish the missing *Mitsvot*, another soul could attach to his soul (*'Ibur*), until he accomplishes it, and then departs. The missing *Mitsva* could be one he chose not to do, or one he could not do in his previous life.

As long as one undertakes the *Tikun* of his soul in three reincarnations, he will come back again as needed to complete his *Tikun*. However, if he maintains his wrong behaviour, he will not come back after the third reincarnation.

The goal of all these complex systems of reincarnation has only one purpose: to allow man to merit by his own efforts, to get closer to his Creator, by perfecting his ways and doing the *Tikun* of his soul.

See Tikun, Neshama

גלגלתא
Gulgolta

First of the three heads of Arikh Anpin

The three heads of *Arikh Anpin* are the roots of the direction of kindness, rigor and mercy. They emanate from *Arikh Anpin* to *Abah* and *Imah,* and from there, to the *Mo'hin* (brains) of *Z"A.*

The first head is *Gulgolta* - It is the *Keter* of *Arikh Anpin.*

גלגלתא לבנה
Gulgolta Levanah

One of the Tikunim of the head of Arikh Anpin

From the head of *Partsuf* (configuration) *Arikh Anpin,* seven emanations come out to act and influence on the guidance, called the *Tikunim* of *Arikh Anpin.*

גמור
Gamur

Complete - Finish *(masculine)*

A *Partsuf* is *Gamur* after the stages of *'Ibur, Yenikah, Leida, Katnut* (gestation, suckling, birth, and infancy)*,* has received all his *Mo'hin* (brains), and is in *Gadlut* (growth) 1 or *Gadlut* 2.

גן עדן
Gan 'Eden

The Garden of Eden

The place of rest for the *Neshamot* (souls) after their separation with their former physical bodies. There is a lower and a higher *Gan 'Eden.*

גן עדן עליון
Gan 'Eden 'Elyon

The upper Garden of Eden

In the higher *Gan 'Eden*, the *Neshamot* (souls) are enjoying pure spiritual pleasures, and do not have any spiritual image resembling their former bodies.

גן עדן תחתון
Gan' Eden Takhton

The lower Garden of Eden

In the lower *Gan 'Eden*, the *Neshamot* (souls) are enjoying spiritual pleasures but still have a spiritual body resembling their former bodies.

גס
Gass

Coarse

The *Klipot* (husks) are by definition of a coarse nature. They get their strength by attaching to the lower *Sephirot* and nourish from the lights of the *Kedushah* (holiness).

See Klipot

גשמיות
Gashmiut

Corporeality

The possibilities of existence for separated entities became possible, only once distanced from the intensity of His light. The greater the distance more is the corporality possible.

Under each world there is a divider, which further diminishes the intensity of the light. Under the divider of the world of *Atsilut*, is the world of *Beriah;* the world of creation, the beginning of existence for the separated; it is the world of the souls. Under the divider of *Beriah,* is the world of *Yetsirah;* the world of formation, the world of the angels. Under the divider of *Yetsirah,* is the world of *'Asiah;* the world of action, the world of corporeality - physical existence.

דבוק
Davuk
Attached - Joined to
Even if they are two distinct *Partsufim* (configurations) and have their own *Tikunim* (actions), all the time that *Partsuf Z"A* is being built, *Partsuf Nukvah* is attached to him.
For the abundance to come down to the world, *Partsuf Zeir Anpin* needs to come to a face to face position and unite with *Nukvah*.

דבקות
Dvekut
Adhesion – Adherence
The goal of all the complex inter-relations and possibilities of guidance, have only one purpose: to allow man to merit by his own efforts, to get closer to his Creator, and live the *Dvekut* – the adhesion with G-od. In this way, man will attain perfection and be directly involved in the ultimate goal of the creation, which is the revelation of *Giluy Ye'hudo* – G-od's Sovereignty.

דו"ן
D"uN
Masculine and feminine
Initials

דוכרין
Dukhrin
Masculine
See Mayin Dukhrin

דוכרין ונוקבין
Dukhrin Ve Nukvin
Masculine and feminine

See Mayin Dukhrin, Mayin Nukvin

דומם
Domem
Inanimate

In parallel to the four worlds of *Atsilut, Beriah, Yetsirah* and *'Asiah,* there are four types of existence in our world: mineral (דומם), vegetal (צומח), animal (חי), and the speaking (מדבר).
Mineral corresponds to the world of *'Asiah.*

דומם, צומח, חי, מדבר
Domem, Tsomeakh, 'Hay, Medaber
Mineral, vegetal, animal and the spoken

In parallel to the four worlds of *Atsilut, Beriah, Yetsirah* and *'Asiah,* there are four types of existence in our world: mineral (דומם), vegetal (צומח), animal (חי), and the speaking (מדבר).
Mineral corresponding to *'Asiah,* vegetal corresponding to *Yetsirah,* animal corresponding to *Beriah,* and the speaking corresponding to *Atsilut.*

דורמיטא
Dormita
Sleep – Somnolence

At first *Partsuf Z"A* is in a state of *Dormita* (somnolence), to act it needs to get his *Mo'hin (brains)* from *Partsuf ISOT* or from *Partsuf Abah* and *Imah,* and to get to a stage of growth.
Inside of *Partsuf Imah, Partsuf Z"A* goes through a period of gestation, followed by a first period of infancy and a first growth. In the first growth his *Mo'hin* are from *NHY (Netsa'h, Hod, Yesod)* of *Partsuf Tevunah.* During the time of the gestation, *Z"A* is not really acting as it is being built, at the time of suckling it starts to act, and at the growth it is ready to act.

דיבור

Dibur

Speech

From the lights that were invested inside of *Adam Kadmon* emerged numerous worlds in the way of his senses; which are called his branches.

These "branches" are the lights that spread forth from *Adam Kadmon,* by way of its apertures in the head, four of which are called: Sight, hearing, smell and speech. They spread out from his eyes, ears, nose, and mouth.

From the mouth came out lights of the aspect of *SaG* (lower *Ta'amim*).

See Orot HaPeh

דין

Din

Rigor – Judgment

At first, the *Ein Sof* (without end) retracted His light from a certain space, and encircled it, so that it would not emanate with its full force. By putting boundaries to his light, He revealed the concepts of rigor and limit needed by the created beings, and gave a space for all the created to exist.

From the *Kav* (ray)*,* ten *Sephirot* were formed in a linear arrangement, and later in three columns: right, left and middle, representing the guidance of the world in the manner of *'Hesed*, *Din* and *Ra'hamim* (Kindness, rigor and mercy).

On the left, the *Din* (rigor) column contains the *Sephirot: Binah*, *Gevurah*, *Hod*.

Some *Partsufim* are masculine and bestow kindness, others are feminine and bestow rigor. By their union, different equilibriums of these two forces (Kindness and rigor), make the guidance. Complete rigor will be the destruction of anything not perfect, while complete kindness will permit everything without restriction. Thus we see that everything that is, and happens, is always composed of a variable measure and balance of these two forces.

Rigor is manifested by all the feminine aspects as: the name of *BaN (52)*, the *Sephira Gevurah,* and by all the concealments of the masculine aspects which represent bounty.

דיקנא
Dikna
Beard (illuminations of the face)
There are hairs (lights) that come out from the face of *Partsuf Arikh Anpin* and *Partsuf Z"A.* They are called *Dikna* (beard), because they spread out in individual conduits.

דם
Dam
Blood
Blood is of the aspect of the *Gevurot (rigors)*, and also contains the *Nefesh (soul).* This is in part why we are not allowed to eat it.

דמות
Demut
Resemblance – Image
Man was created to the image of the *Sephirot* and *Partsufim.*
See Partsuf

דעת
Da'at
Sephira (Knowledge)
Fourth of the *Sephirot.*
Da'at is counted when *Keter* is not.

Quality: Guidance that makes the equilibrium between *'Hokhma and Binah*.

Column: Middle – *'Ra'hamim* (mercy)

Position: Middle – center

Other *Sephirot* on the same column: *Keter, Tiferet, Yesod, Malkhut*

Partsufim made from this *Sephira: none, but from it come out the five 'Hasadim and five Gevurot.* Its role is mainly to make the *Mo'hin* for *Z"A* and *Nukvah*.

Corresponding name: *AHV-H –* אהו-ה

See Sephira, Partsuf

דעת

Da'at

Knowledge

The essential knowledge is the one of the will of the Creator and His ways of guidance in this existence, as explained in the Kabbalah.

דק

Dak

Thin - Fine – Tenuous

When the *Sephirot* came out the first time from the mouth of *Adam Kadmon,* only the most tenuous part of the lights returned to their origin in the mouth.

See Orot HaPeh

דרך

Derekh

Way

Direction. In the manner of.

ה' אלעה
Hey Ela'a
Higher (ה) Hey
First H (ה) of the Tetragamon (י-ה-ו-ה) *B'H,* corresponds to *Partsuf Imah.*

ה' תתאה
Hey Tataa
Lower (ה) Hey
Second H (ה) of the Tetragamon (י-ה-ו-ה) *B'H,* corresponds to *Sephira Malkhut.*

הארה
Hearah
Illumination
Special outburst of a light for a specific purpose.

הבדל
Hevdel
Difference – Change
There are differences in the emanations of the lights depending on their importance or position.
Each *Sephira* is composed of a vessel called *Keli,* which holds its part of light called *Or.* There is no difference in the *Or* itself, which is a unique emanation form G-od; the difference comes from the particularity, or quality of the *Sephira.*

הבלא דגרמי
Habela Degarmi
The *Or* (light) that gives life to the *Keli* (recipient) is comparable to the soul that keeps the body alive. When a man dies and his soul separates from his body, the latter will remain with the

"*Habela Degarmi* "(הבלא דגרמי) which like the 288 sparks, will allow the conservation of the body from the time the soul has left him, until the resurrection.

See Rapa'h Netsutsot

ההין
HaHin
Of ה (H)
When the letter ה is used to make the *Miluy* (spelling).

הוד
Hod
Sephira – Glory
Eighth of the *Sephirot*.
Quality: Diminished rigor to who is deserving.
Column: Left – *Din* (rigor)
Position: Left – bottom
Other *Sephirot* on the same column: *Binah, Gevurah.*
Partsufim made from this *Sephira:*
One of the *Sephirot* that make the *Partsuf Z"A.*
Corresponding name: *Elohi-m Tsebaot*
אלהי-ם -צבאות
Corresponding *Miluy* of name: *MaH (45)* (מה)
Corresponding vowel: *Kubutz*
Physical correspondance: Left leg
Level of the soul: *Rua'h*
See Sephira, Partsuf

הוי"ה
HaVaYaH
One of the ways of mentioning the Tetragamon
יְ-ה-ו-ה without pronouncing it.

הולדה

Olada

Giving birth

One of the steps in the *Tikun* (repair – rectification) of a *Partsuf* (configuration). After the gestation inside the superior feminine *Partsuf Nukvah*, the *Partsuf* comes out and continues his growth process.

היכלות

Hekhalot

Portals – Levels

See Hekhal

היכל

Hekhal

Portal – Level

Each world (*ABYA*) is built from four aspects: *Partsuf* (configuration), *Levush* (garment), *Or Makif* (encircling lights), and *Hekhalot* (portals).

The principal function of the *Hekhalot* is to allow the adhesion and attachment, to ascend in various ways, until the seventh highest *Hekhal (portal) Kodesh Hakodashim*.

The *Hekhalot* are also the different levels of ascension of the *Tefilot* before reaching the *'Olam Atsilut* during the *Amidah*.

	Hekhal / Portal	**Corresponding to**
First	לבנת הספיר	*Yesod* and *Malkhut*
	(*Livnat Hasapir*)	
Second	עצם השמים	*Hod*
	(*'Etsem Hashamayim*)	

87

Third	נוגה (Nogah)	Netsa'h
Fourth	זכות (Zekhut)	Gevurah
Fifth	אהבה (Ahavah)	'Hesed
Sixth	רצון (Ratson)	Tiferet
Seventh	קדש קדשים (Kodesh Kodashim)	Keter, 'Hokhma, Binah

The goal of the service of the creatures, is to help prepare the *Partsufim Z"A* and *Nukvah* for the *Zivug (union),* and this, by the elevation and adhesion of the worlds of *Beriah*, *Yetsirah* and *'Asiah* to the *Hekhalot* of *Nukvah* of *Atsilut.*

See Kavanah

הכללי
HaKlali
One of the seven main types of *Gematriot.*
The *Ragil* value of the word squared.
Ex : הארץ = 296 * 296 = 87616
See Gematria

הכנה
Hakhana
Preparation
The word Kabbalah comes from the verb *Lekabel* (to receive), but to receive it is first necessary to be prepared, and to be a *Keli* (recipient) able to receive and contain this knowledge.
See Tefilah, Mitsvot

הכפלה
Hakhpalah
Increase
There are increases in the size of the *Sephirot* or *Partsufim*

(configurations) *Z"A* and *Nukvah,* depending on their growth stage.

See Gadlut

המשכה
Hamshakhah
Drawing – Extension
For the *Tikun* (rectification), the lower feminine lights ascend and draw to them the masculine higher lights.

המתקה
Hamtakah
Mitigation – Sweetening
A mitigation or sweetening of the *Gevurot* (rigors) occurs when they are in direct contact with the *'Hasadim.*

הנהגה
Hanhagah
Guidance
The Kabbalah is the only science that explains to us in the least details, the true guidance of the world, so that we may understand His will. It teaches us that the world is guided by an extremely complex system of forces or lights, which through their interactions provoke chain reactions that impact directly on man and the guidance of the worlds. Each one of these reactions has numerous ramifications with many details and results.

The guidance of the worlds is done through the influence of the different *Sephirot* and *Partsufim (configurations).*

There are two main kinds of guidance:

The general guidance, which is for the subsistence of the worlds, and is not influenced by the actions of men. This guidance is by the encircling *Sephirot.*

The variable guidance, which is on the basis of justice, reward and punishment, is dependant on the actions of man. This guidance is by the linear *Sephirot*.

The linear *Sephirot* are arranged in three columns: right, left and middle, representing the guidance of the world in the manner of *'Hesed, Din* and *Ra'hamim* - Kindness, rigor and mercy.

The guidance of the world is dependent on the different positioning and interaction of the masculine and feminine *Partsufim (configuration)*, since they have a direct effect on the measure and balance of the factors of kindness, rigor and mercy.

The masculine *Partsufim (configurations)* bestow kindness, the feminine bestow rigor. By their union, different equilibriums of the two forces of kindness and rigor make the guidance. Complete rigor will be the destruction of anything not perfect, while complete kindness will permit everything without restriction. However, these two aspects are necessary for the guidance of justice, and to give man the possibility of free choice

See Sephirot, Partsuf, Tikun, Sephira

הפרעות

Hafra'ot

Disturbance

Disturbance is caused by the increase of the *Klipot* (husks) or in the absence of *Kedushah* (Holiness).

הפרתי

HaPerati

One of the seven main types of *Gematriot*.

Each letter is squared.

Ex : הארץ = 5 * 5 = 25, 1 * 1 = 1,

200 * 200 = 40 000,   900 * 900 = 810 000

Total = 850 026

הקדמי

HaKadmi

One of the seven main types of *Gematriot*.

Each letter has its *Ragil* value plus the total of all the ones preceding it.

From	To	Value
א	ט	1 - 45
י	צ	55 – 495
ק	ת	595 – 1495
ך	ץ	1995 – 4995

Ex : הארץ = 15 + 1 + 795 + 4995 = 5806

See Gematria

הרחקה

Har'hakah

Distancing

Distance denotes a contrary or a non compatibility.

The possibilities of existence for separated entities became possible, only once distanced from the intensity of His light.

See Tsimtsum, A'hor Be A'hor

השגה

Hasagah

Attainment - Comprehension

To reach a higher level of understanding or comprehension, one has to make the effort of studying the *Sod* (secret) of the Torah which is the Kabbalah.

See Kabbalah, Torah

השוואה

Hashavah

Equivalence

Depending on time, the masculine and feminine *Partsufim* (configurations) vary in size. The ideal is when the *Zivug* (union) is done when these *Partsufim* are equivalent in size.

See Zivug

השפעה

Hashpa'ah

Bestowal

At first, the Creator was alone, occupying all space with His light. His light without end, borders or limit, filled everything. He was not bestowing His influence, because there was no one to receive it. When He willed to create, He started to influence.

Since the intention of the Creator is to bestow goodness on His creatures, all the levels of creation were put in place so His kindness could emanate to them, yet in such a way that they would be able to receive it.

All and everything is sustained by one and only one source; the light of G-od, which is bestowed through these *Partsufim* and *Sephirot*.

See Ratson Lehashpia'

השתלשלות

Hishtalshelut

Evolution - Chain of events

In the Kabbalah the *Hishtalshelut* is the chain of events starting from the first act of G-od in this creation which is the "*Tsimtsum*" *(retraction)*, until the complex arrangements that make the guidance of the worlds.

See Tsmitsum, Kav, Sephirot

התעבות

Hit'abot

Thickening

From *Adam Kadmon*, different emanations spread out as a preparation for the future worlds. One of these first emanations came out from its mouth; these lights did not find an individual *Keli* (recipient) and returned to their origin in the mouth. They did not return completely, only the most tenuous part did, each one leaving its trace. The parts that remained thickened, but were still illuminated by their own parts that ascended.

See Shvirat HaKelim

התפשטות

Hitpashtut

Spreading

After entering, the different lights spread down.

For *Adam Kadmon*, lights spread forth from him by way of its apertures in the head and are called his "branches".

Inside *Partsuf Z"A*, *'Hasadim* spread and rise until *Keter,* before he attaines the growth level.

See Adam Kadmon, Mo'hin

ויהוא"ל
Vihue"l
Name of one of the three great princes of the Angels.

ויטאל
Vital
Rabbi 'Haim Vital
Born in Tsfat in 1543, died in Damascus in 1620.
Main student of the Ari Z'al. During the two years that the Ari lived in Tsfat, Rabbi 'Haim Vital studied with him the Kabbalah. After the passing of the Ari, he put all of his teachings in writing in what is called the "Kitve HaAri" (the Writings of the Ari).

וילנא
Vilna
Rabbi Eliyahu of Vilna - The Gaon of Vilna
Born in Vilna, Lithuania, 1720, died in Vilna in 1797.
One of the main leaders of the Mitnagdim (opponents to the 'Hasidic movement). Some of his works on the Kabbalah are called "Kitvei HaGra Be'eniene Kabbalah"

ולד
Valad
Child - Infant – Fetus
All the *Tikunim* of the masculine and feminine *Partsufim (configurations)* are achieved by way of *Zivug* (union), gestation and birth. During the *Zivug*, the lights of *MaH (45)* needed for the *Tikun* are drawn to the lights of *BaN (52)*, and are kept in the upper *Nukvah*. During the gestation, inside of *Nukvah*, they are arranged and completed until there is nothing more to add. When it is totally repaired, the *Partsuf* is born or revealed, and this is the birth.

ז' מלכים

Sheva' Malkhin

Seven kings

The seven kings of Edom that died (Bereshit, 36, 31), correspond to the seven lower *Sephirot* that broke during the *Shvirat HaKelim* (breaking of the vessels).

See Shvirat HaKelim

ז"א

Z"A

Zeir Anpin (Small countenance)

Initials of *Partsuf Zeir Anpin*, used more often than the full name.

See Zeir Anpin

ז"ת

Za"T

Zain Takhtonot

Initials of the seven lower *Sephirot*

זו"ן

Z"UN

Zeir Anpin and Nukvah

Initials of *Partsuf Zeir Anpin and Nukvah*, used more often than the full names.

זוהמא

Zohama

Filth – Foulness

State of distance from he *Kedushah* and closeness to the *Sitra A'hra (negative force)*.

See *Sitra A'hra*

זוהר
Zohar
The book of splendor, written by Rabbi Shim'on Bar Yo'hay.
The *Zohar* is the esoteric and mystical explanation of the Torah, and the base for most of the Kabbalah writings.
See Bar Yo'hay

זווג דנשיקין
Zivug De Neshikin
Union of the kisses
There are two types of unions for the *Zivug* (unions): the kissing and the *Yesodot* (by the *Sephira Yesod*). The kissing is to attach the interiority of the masculine with the one of the feminine. The *Yesodot* is to attach the exteriority of the masculine with the one of the feminine.
See Zivug, Tikun

זווג של יסודות
Zivug shel Yesodot
Union of the Yesodot
There are two types of unions for the *Zivug* (unions): the kissing and the *Yesodot* (by the *Sephira Yesod*). The kissing is to attach the interiority of the masculine with the one of the feminine. The *Yesodot* is to attach the exteriority of the masculine with the one of the feminine.
The second of the two steps for the *Zivug*, is the *Zivug* of the *Yesodot* (by the two *Sephirot Yesod*), it completes the *Zivug,* and it is from this *Zivug* that emanations are spread to the worlds.

זיו
Ziv
Radiance – Illumination

A superior light will illuminate to a lower one to influence it, or to create a new emanation.

זיווג
Zivug
Union
The *Zivug* is the union of the masculine with its feminine. All the outcomes of the higher emanations are a result of the different unions of the masculine and feminine lights.

There are different kinds of *Zivugim*; the ones for the construction of the worlds, for the building of the *Partsufim*, and for the guidance of the worlds.

For the abundance to come down to the world, *Partsuf Zeir Anpin* needs to unite with *Nukvah (Ra'hel or Leah)*. There can be abundance only when the masculine and the feminine are in harmony. Each day, according to the actions of man, the *Tefilot* (prayers) during the week, *Shabbat* or holidays and depending on time, various configurations allow different *Zivugim*, and therefore outflows of abundance of variable intensities.

There are five different *Zivugim*:
- The *Zivugim* with *Ra'hel* are of the highest level; being of the aspect of kindness.
- The ones with *Leah* are more of the aspect of rigor.
- The one of *Israel* and *Ra'hel* is the most superior. *Israel* represents all of *Z"A*, *Ra'hel* is the essential of *Nukvah*. The abundance that is bestowed by this *Zivug* is the most complete.
- The other *Zivugim* of *Z"uN* are of different levels, in various times, and of lesser plenitude.

Each new day, is of a new emanation that governs it. For each day, there are new *Zivugim* of different aspects of *Z"uN*.

- In the *Tefilah* (prayer) of *Sha'hrit*, there is the *Zivug* of *Ya'acov* and *Ra'hel*
- In the *Tefilah* of *Min'ha*, there is the *Zivug* of *Israel* and *Leah.*
- In the *Tefilah* of *'Arvit*, there is the *Zivug* of *Ya'acov* and *Leah* (from the chest up).
- In *Tikun 'Hatsot*, there is the *Zivug* of *Ya'acov* and *Leah* (from the chest down).

The guidance of the world is dependent on the different positioning and interaction, of these masculine and feminine *Partsufim*, since they have a direct effect on the measure and balance of the factors of kindness, rigor and mercy.

The goal of the service of the creatures, is to help prepare the *Partsufim Z"A* and *Nukvah* for the *Zivug,* and this, by the elevation and adhesion of the worlds by way of the *Tefilot* and *Mitsvot.*

זיווגים

Zivugim

Unions

See Zivug

זין תחתונות

Zayin Takhtonot

Seven lower

The seven lower *Sephirot:*

'Hesed, Gevurah, Tiferet, Netsa'h, Hod, Yesod, Malkhut.

See Partsuf Zeir Anpin

זך

Zakh

Tenuous - Refined

In general when a light needs to ascend, its most tenuous part will go up, and the remaining will "thicken" being now separated from its more tenuous part.

זכות

Zekhut

Name of a *Hekhal (portal)*.

Fourth of seven *Hekhalot*, corresponding to *Gevurah*.

The *Hekhalot* are the different levels of ascension of the *Tefilot* (prayers) before reaching the final seventh *Hekhal* (portal); *Kodesh Hakodashim*.

זכר

Zakhar

Masculine

There are masculine *Partsufim* that bestow kindness, and feminine *Partsufim* that bestow rigor. By their union, different equilibriums of these two forces (kindness and rigor), make the guidance. Kindness is manifested by all the masculine aspects which represent bounty, and by the concealment of the feminine aspects, which represent rigor.

The *Zivug* is the union of the masculine with its feminine. All the outcomes of the higher emanations are a result of the different unions of the masculine and feminine lights.

The masculine corresponds to *'Hesed* and *MaH (45)*, the feminine to *Gevurah* and *BaN (52)*. The *Tikun* is only possible by the *Zivug* (union) of the masculine and the feminine.

The guidance of the world is dependent on the different positioning and interaction, of the masculine and feminine

Partsufim, since they have a direct effect on the measure and balance of the factors of kindness, rigor and mercy.

See Zivug, Tikun, Zeir Anpin

זמן
Zman

Time

Each day, according to the actions of man, the *Tefilot* during the week, *Shabbat* or holidays, and depending on time, various configurations allow different *Zivugim*, and therefore outflows of abundance of variable intensities.

Each moment can also be described in term of permutation of the names of G-od, and by the various *Sephirot and Partsufim*.

זמנים
Zmanim

Times

See Zman

זעיר אנפין
Zeir Anpin

Partsuf Zeir Anpin (Small countenance)

Zeir Anpin (Z"A) is composed of the seven lower *Sephirot:* *'Hesed, Gevurah, Tiferet, Netsa'h, Hod, Yesod* and *Malkhut* of a world.

At first *Z"A* is in a state of *Tardema* (somnolence), to act he needs to get his *Mo'hin (brains),* which are his first three *Sephirot* of *"Hokhma, Binah* and *Da'at* from *ISOT* or *Abah* and *Imah*, and to get to a stage of growth.

For the abundance to come down to the world, *Zeir Anpin* needs to unite with *Nukvah*. There can be abundance only when the masculine and the feminine are in harmony. Each day, according

100

to the actions of man, the *Tefilot* (prayers) during the week, *Shabbat* or holidays and depending on time, various configurations allow different *Zivugim*, and therefore outflows of abundance of variable intensities. The abundance first comes to *Z"A*, then to *Nukvah,* and from her, to the lower worlds.

There are five different *Zivugim*, the *Zivugim* with *Ra'hel* are of the highest level; being of the aspect of kindness, the ones with Leah are more of the aspect of rigor. The one of *Israel* and *Ra'hel* is the most superior. *Israel* represents all of *Z"A*, *Ra'hel* is the essential of *Nukvah*. The abundance that is bestowed by this *Zivug (union)* is the most complete. The other *Zivugim* are of different levels, in various times, and of lesser plenitude.

Each new day, is of a new emanation that governs it. For each day, there are new *Zivugim* of different aspects of *Z"uN*. The guidance of the world is dependent on the different positioning and interaction, of *Z"A* and *Nukvah*, since they have a direct effect on the measure and balance of the factors of kindness, rigor and mercy.

The goal of the service of the creatures, is to help prepare the *Partsufim (configurations) Z"A* and *Nukvah* for the *Zivug (union),* and this by the elevation and adhesion of the worlds by way of the *Tefilot* and *Mitsvot*.
See Partsuf, Tikun, Zivug, Sephira

זקן
Zakan

Beard
The beard *(Zakan)* is also called *Dikna* and is the illuminations that come out from the face.
See Dikna

חבד
'HaBaD
'Hokhma, Binah and Da'at
Initials of the first triplet of the *Sephirot: 'Hokhma, Binah and Da'at*. They act together as *Mo'hin* (brains) for a lower *Partsuf* and are called the *Mo'hin* of *Gadlut* (growth).\

חגת
'HaGaT
'Hesed, Gevurah and Tiferet
Initials of the second triplet of the *Sephirot: 'Hesed, Gevurah and Tiferet*. They mostly act together as *Mo'hin* (brains) for a lower *Partsuf*.

חוורתי
'Hivarti
The white on the scalp between the hair
From the *Partsuf (configuration) Arikh Anpin* there are emanations that come out from its head to act and influence on the guidance called the *Tikunim* of *Arikh Anpin*.
One of these *Tikunim* of *Arikh Anpin* is from his *Keter* and is the *'Hivarti*; they are the white parts between each hair.

חולם
'Holam – Vowel O
The vowel that represents the *Sephira Tiferet*.

חומר
'Homer
Material – Physical
Materiality is only found in the lower world of *'Asiah* – action.

102

חוץ
'Huts
Outside
Denotes a position of non-compatibility or a contrary.

חושך
'Hoshekh
Darkness
State of distance from the *Kedushah* and closeness to the *Sitra A'hra* (negative side).

חותם
'Hotam
Seal
Represented by the Name *Shada-y* - שד-י

חותמא
'Hotma
Seventh of seven Tikunim of the head of Arikh Anpin
From the head of *Partsuf* (configuration) *Arikh Anpin,* seven emanations come out to act and influence on the guidance, called the *Tikunim* of *Arikh Anpin.*

חזה
'Hazeh
Chest
The chest corresponds to the first third of the *Sephira Tiferet*. In general the lights will enter until the chest, or lower to the navel.

חיבוק
'Hibuk
Embrace
Before the *Zivug* (union) of the *Yesodot*.

חיבור

'Hibur

Attachment

All the *Sephirot* and *Partsufim* have a certain degree of attachment between them. Even if they are two distinct *Partsufim* (configurations) and have their own *Tikunim* (actions), all the time that *Partsuf Z"A* is being built, *Partsuf Nukvah* is attached to him.

For their livelihood, the negative forces get strength by attaching to the exteriority of the *Sephirot*. They nourish from their lights and gain more power to act negatively.

There are also other temporary attachments as body and soul, interiority and exteriority etc.

See Partsufim

חידוש

'Hidush

Innovation

New interpretation or new understanding.

חיה

'Hayah

Fourth level of the soul

The soul has five names: *Nefesh*, *Rua'h*, *Neshama*, *'Hayah* and *Ye'hidah*, which correspond to its five levels. The soul is the spiritual entity inside the body, the latter being only his outer garment.

Since it is men that provoke the union of the four worlds, it is necessary for their souls to have their origin from them, and from the five *Partsufim*:

Soul / Level	Partsuf	World
Nefesh	Nukvah	'Asiah
Rua'h	Zeir Anpin	Yetsirah
Neshama	Imah	Beriah
'Hayah	Abah	Atsilut
Ye'hidah	Arikh Anpin	Atsilut

Each level of the soul is subdivided in five levels. As for the level
of *Nefesh;* there are *Nefesh* of *Nefesh, Rua'h* of *Nefesh,
Neshama* of *Nefesh,* '*Hayah* of *Nefesh* and *Ye'hidah* of *Nefesh.*
Each one of these levels of the soul subdivides for each level of
Partsuf and for each world.   Therefore, there are five levels of the
souls for *Partsuf Nukvah* and there are five levels of *Partsufim* for
the world of *'Asiah* etc. Also, as there are in each world ten
Sephirot, each soul has its origin corresponding to one of them.
Therefore, a soul could be from the level of *Nefesh* of *Malkhut* of
Nukvah of *'Asiah,* or *Rua'h* of *'Hesed* of *Abah* of *'Yetsirah,* or
Neshama of *Abah* of *Z"A* of *Yetsirah* etc.

'Hayah is the fourth level and can only be acquired after the
preceding levels.
The higher levels of the soul cannot be acquired at once. Most
men only have the level of *Nefesh,* and if they merit, they will
acquire the next levels - but one by one. To reach the next higher
level of his soul, man must do the *Tikun* of the preceding level. If
he needs to acquire the level of *Imah* of *'Asiah,* he must first do
the *Tikun* of *Malkhut* of *'Asiah* and *Z"A* of *'Asiah,* and so on. To
acquire his level of *Neshama,* he must do the *Tikun* of all the
levels of the *Sephirot* and *Partsufim* of his *Nefesh* and *Rua'h etc.*

חיות
'Hayut
Livelihood
The livelihood of everything, whether positive or negative has only one origin; G-od the Creator and sustainer of all.

חיצון
'Hitson
Exterior
As there are interior aspects, there are also exterior aspects. All the lights subdivide among themselves in interiority and exteriority aspects. Depending on the context, the exterior aspect could be superior or opposite to the interior aspect.

חיצוניות
'Hitsoniut
Exteriority (The)
There are different types of exteriority. The exteriority of a world is its inferior aspect. The exteriority could also be a contrary or opposite, and is in general inferior to the interiority.
As the *Neshama* is the interiority, and the body exteriority, so is also the *Kav* interiority and *Reshimu* exteriority etc. The *Malkhuts* of the *Sephirot,* which are their lower level, are called their exteriority.
The external or negative force – *Sitra A'hra* is also called the exteriority.
See Sitra A'hra

חיריק
'Hirik – Vowel I
The vowel that represents the *Sephira Netsa'h*

חכמה

'Hokhma

Sephira – Wisdom

Second of the *Sephirot.*

Quality: Kindness to all, even to the not deserving (but less than *Keter,* and not always).

Column: Right – '*Hesed* (Kindness)

Position: Top – right

Other *Sephirot* on the same column: '*Hesed, Netsa'h.*

Partsufim made from this *Sephira:*

- *Abah*

- From *Malkhut* of *Abah* - *Israel Saba*

- From *Malkhut* of *Israel Saba* - *Israel Saba 2*

Corresponding name: *YH* ה-י

Corresponding *Miluy* (spelling) of name: *'A"V* - עב *(72)*

Corresponding vowel: *Pata'h*

Physical correspondence: Right brain
Level of the soul: *'Hayah*

See Sephira, Partsuf

חכמה

'Hokhma

Wisdom – Intelligence – Knowledge
"The beginning of wisdom is to awe (venerate)
G-od."*(Tehilim 111, 10)*

חכמת האמת

'Hokhmat HaEmet

Knowledge of the truth
One of the names of the Kabbalah.

חלל

'Hallal

Space – Vacuum

The space left by the *Tsimtsum* (retraction) of His light. This space is circular and contains all possibilities of existence for separated entities, since they are distanced from the intensity of His light.

See Tsimtsum, Kav, Reshimu

חסד

'Hesed

Bounty - Kindness

Since the intention of the Creator is to bestow goodness on His creatures, all the levels of creation were put in place so His kindness could emanate to them, yet in such a way that they would be able to receive it.

From the *Kav (ray of His light),* ten *Sephirot* were formed in a linear arrangement, and later in three columns: right, left and middle, representing the guidance of the world in the manner of *'Hesed, Din* and *Ra'hamim* (Kindness, rigor and mercy). This guidance is dependent on time, and the actions of men.

For the emanation of Kindness, there are various *Tikunim* (actions) of the *Sephirot* and *Partsufim.* Some *Partsufim* are masculine and bestow kindness, others are feminine and bestow rigor. By their union, different equilibriums of the two forces of Kindness and rigor make the guidance. Complete rigor will be the destruction of anything not perfect, while complete kindness will permit everything without restriction.

Kindness is manifested by the different positioning and interaction of these masculine and feminine *Partsufim,* since they have a direct effect on the measure and balance of the factors of kindness, rigor and mercy.

108

חסד

'Hesed

Sephira (Bounty)

Fourth of the *Sephirot.*

Quality: Complete kindness to who is deserving.

Column: Right – *'Hesed* (kindness)

Position: Right – Middle

Other *Sephirot* on the same column: *'Hokhma, Netsa'h.*

Partsufim made from this *Sephira:*

One of the *Sephirot* that make the *Partsuf Z"A.*

Corresponding name: *El* – אל

Corresponding *Miluy* (spelling) of name *MaH (45)* (מה)

Corresponding vowel: *Segol*

Physical correspondence: Right arm

Level of the soul: *Rua'h*

חסד, גבורה, תפארת

'Hesed, Gevurah and Tiferet

Second triplet of the *Sephirot,* they correspond to the right and left arm, and the body. They mostly act together as *Mo'hin* (brains) for a lower *Partsuf.*

חסדים

'Hasadim

Kindnesses

For the guidance five emanations of the aspect of *'Hesed* (kindness) and five emanations of the aspect of *Gevurah* (rigors), are given by the *Sephira Da'at* to the *Partsufim* (configurations) *Z"A* and *Nukvah. Partsuf Z"A* receives the five *'Hasadim* and *Nukvah* receives the five *Gevurot.*

After the complete spreading of the *'Hasadim* in *Partsuf Z"A,* and their rise until *Keter, Partsuf Z"A* has attained the growth level.

חסרון

'Hisaron

Lack – deficiency

State of distance from the *Kedushah* and closeness to the *Sitra A'hra (negative force)*.

חפירה

'Hafirah

Digging – Deepening

Term used as analyzing and deepening the first levels of understanding.

חשוב

'Hashuv

Important

See *'Hashivut*

חשיבות

'Hashivut

Importance

All the worlds are similar; they all contain ten *Sephirot* and five *Partsufim*, but the higher is more complete and important than the one under it.

There is also a difference of importance in the position and the various emanations of the lights, *Sephirot* and *Partsufim*.

See *Sephirot, Partsufim*

ט' ראשונות

Tet Rishonot

First Nine

First nine *Sephirot: Keter, 'Hokhma, Binah, 'Hesed, Gevurah, Tiferet, Netsa'h, Hod, Yesod.*

טבור

Tabur

Navel

The navel corresponds to the second third of *Tiferet*. In general the lights will enter until the chest, or lower to the level of the navel.

טל

Tal

Thirty nine

Miluy (spelling) of the name י - ה - ו

יוד הא ואו = 39 .

טלא דבדולחא

Tela Debadul'ha

Second of the seven Tikunim of the head of Arikh Anpin

From the head of *Partsuf* (configuration) *Arikh Anpin*, seven emanations come out to act and influence on the guidance, called the *Tikunim* of *Arikh Anpin*.

טלית

Talit - Praying shawl

The *Talit* represents the *Or Makif* (encircling light).

טמא

Tameh

Impure

State of distance from the *Kedushah* and closeness to the *Sitra*

A'hra (negative force).

טנת"א
TaNTA
Ta'amim, Nekudot, Tagin, and Autiot.
Initials

טעמים
Ta'amim
Cantillation notes
From the lights that were invested inside of Adam Kadmon emerged numerous worlds in the way of his senses; which are called his branches. These "branches" are the lights that spread forth from Adam Kadmon, by way of its apertures in the head. They spread out from his eyes, ears, nose, and mouth.

From the aspect of the name "A"V of SaG, came out three branches in the aspects of the Ta'amim (cantillation). They came out through the ears, nose, and mouth: the higher from the ears, the middle from the nose, and the lower from the mouth.
See Orot HaOzen. Orot Ha'Hotem, Orot HaPeh

טעמים, נקודות, תגין, אותיות
Ta'amim, Nekudot, Tagin, and Autiot.
Cantillation signs, vowels, crowns and letters.
From the lights that were invested inside Adam Kadmon, emerged numerous worlds in the way of his senses; which are called his branches. These "branches" are the lights that spread forth from Adam Kadmon, by way of its apertures in the head. They spread out from his eyes, ears, nose, mouth and forehead.

The Ta'amim (cantillation marks) are of the highest level and are subdivided in three: higher, middle and lower. The Nekudot (vowels) are second, also in three levels: higher, middle and lower. The *Tagin* (crowns) are third, and appear on top of some letters only. The *Autiot* (letters) are fourth.

The reading of the Torah is incomplete without the *Ta'amim*, *Nekudot*, *Tagin,* and *Autiot*. The *Autiot* are the expression of the *Ma'hshava* (thought). In combination with the *Ta'amim*, *Nekudot*, *Tagin,* or with other letters, they transform the higher lights into action.

טפל

Taffel

Subordinate - Accessory

The *Taffel* is always subordinate to the *'Ikar*, which is the main or the essential. Some emanations are subordinate to other more important lights.

י-ה
YaH
YH
One of the names of G-od, represented by the *Sephira 'Hokhma.*

י-ה ו ה
Adona-y
Y-H-V-H *Tetragamon* (י-ה-ו-ה)
Main name of G-od, reveals kindness and mercy, represented by the *Sephira Tiferet.*
The creative forces or energies are the different powers in the letters of the name of G-od י-ה-ו-ה, and the various letters added to make their different spellings. Depending on which letters are used, the numerical value of the name changes, and each one of these possibilities becomes different in its nature and actions.
The lights or forces that are clothed in these letters or their combinations emanate masculine or feminine configurations that make the guidance of the worlds.
See Mlluy

י ה -ו-ה צבאות
Adona-y Tsebaot
Y-H-V-H Tsebaot
One of the names of G-od, represented by the *Sephira Netsa'h.*

יודין
Yudin
Of the letter ' (yud)
Miluy (spelling) when the letter ' *(yud) is used.*
See 'A"V

114

יום

Yom

Day

Each new day, is of a new emanation that governs it. For each day, there are new *Zivugim* (unions) of different aspects of *Z"uN* (*Zeir Anpin and Nukvah*).

Each day, according to the actions of man, the *Tefilot* during the week, *Shabbat* or Holidays, and depending on time, various configurations allow different *Zivugim*, and therefore outflows of abundance of variable intensities.

Each day can also be described in term of permutation of the names of G-od, and by the various *Sephirot and Partsufim* that govern on this day.

יוסף

Yoseph

Corresponds to the *Sephira Yesod*.

יוצר

Yotser

Creator

G-od the one and only Creator.

יחוד

Yi'hud

Unification – Union

The union of the *Sephirot* or *Partsufim* for the *Zivug* and for the descent of the abundance.

A *Yi'hud* is the unification of names or letters, as to provoke a specific action or reaction. In his book "*Sha'ar Rua'h HaKodesh*" the Ari Z'al explains the significance of the *Yi'hudim*, their different actions, and also warns of the danger of using these names without a proper preparation. By concentrating on various permutation of letters or names of angels, one could make these superior forces act according to his will.

There is also the revelation of the *Yi'hud* (unicity) of G-od. At the end of times, after all the *Tikunim*, it will be time for the *Moshia'h* to reveal himself, and all the world will see this complete unification to G-od's perfection caused by the revelation of His truth; which is the ultimate goal of the creation.

See Giluy Yi'hudo

יחודו

Yi'hudo

His unicity

The light of G-od is unique, of equal force, quality and beyond all description. It is perfect, and cannot be measured by any definition or limiting terms. If we think about definitions, we introduce a notion of limit or absence of its opposite. However, the concept of limitlessness is beyond our human comprehension, and we therefore have to use terms accessible to our understanding. Being ourselves distinct separate beings, we cannot grasp the concept of the "non-distinct", everything we know is finite, by having a measure or an opposite. When we use terms as 'quality', it is to differentiate the various transformations of His unicity when it is at our level, and to help us understand its effects upon the guidance of the worlds.

At the end of times, after all the *Tikunim* (rectifications), it will be time for the *Moshia'h* to reveal himself. All the world will see the complete unification to G-od's perfection by the revelation of His truth.

The aim is to allow man to merit by his own efforts, to get closer to his Creator, and live the *Dvekut* – the adhesion with G-od. In this way, man will attain perfection and be directly involved in the

ultimate goal of this existence, which is the revelation of G-od's
Unicity and Sovereignty – *Giluy Ye'hudo.*

יחודים
Yi'hudim
Unifications – Unions
See Yi'hud

יחיד ומיוחד
Ya'hid Umeyu'had
One and Unique
Can only apply to G-od.
See E'had, Yi'hudo

יחידה
Ye'hidah
Fifth level of the soul
The soul has five names: *Nefesh, Rua'h, Neshama, 'Hayah* and
Ye'hidah, which correspond to its five levels. The soul is the
spiritual entity inside the body, the latter being only his outer
garment.
Since it is men that provoke the union of the four worlds, it is
necessary for their souls to have their origin from them, and from
the five *Partsufim*:

Soul / Level	Partsuf	World
Nefesh	Nukvah	'Asiah
Rua'h	Zeir Anpin	Yetsirah
Neshama	Imah	Beriah
'Hayah	Abah	Atsilut
Ye'hidah	Arikh Anpin	Atsilut

Each level of the soul is subdivided in five levels. As for the level of *Nefesh;* there are *Nefesh* of *Nefesh, Rua'h* of *Nefesh, Neshama* of *Nefesh, 'Hayah* of *Nefesh* and *Ye'hidah* of *Nefesh.*

Each one of these levels of the soul subdivides for each level of *Partsuf* and for each world. Therefore, there are five levels of the souls for *Partsuf Nukvah* and there are five levels of *Partsufim* for the world of *'Asiah* etc. Also, as there are in each world ten *Sephirot*, each soul has its origin corresponding to one of them.

Therefore, a soul could be from the level of *Nefesh* of *Malkhut* of *Nukvah* of *'Asiah,* or *Rua'h* of *'Hesed* of *Abah* of *'Yetsirah,* or *Neshama* of *Abah* of *Z"A* of *Yetsirah* etc.

Ye'hidah is the fifth level and can only be acquired after the preceding levels.

The higher levels of the soul cannot be acquired at once. Most men only have the level of *Nefesh,* and if they merit, they will acquire the next levels - but one by one. To reach the next higher level of his soul, man must do the *Tikun* of the preceding level.

ימים

Yamim

Days

See Yom

יניקה

Yenikah

Suckling

All the *Tikunim (rectifications)* of the masculine and feminine *Partsufim (configurations)* are achieved by way of *Zivug* (union), gestation and birth. Afterwards, is the suckling and finally the growth for the *Partsuf* to be fully independent.

See Gadlut

118

יסוד

Yesod

Sephira (Foundation)

Ninth of the *Sephirot*.

Quality: Guidance that makes the equilibrium between *Sephira Netsa'h and Hod.*

Link or connection between all the superior *Sephirot* and *Malkhut.*

Column: Center – *Ra'hamim* (mercy)

Position: Middle – Bottom

Other *Sephirot* on the same column: *Keter, Tiferet, Malkhut*

Partsufim made from this *Sephira:*

One of the *Sephirot* that make the *Partsuf Z"A.*

Corresponding name: *Shada- y* -- שד-י

Corresponding *Miluy* (spelling) of name: *MaH* -מה *(45)*

Corresponding vowel: *Shirik*

Physical correspondence: Masculine organ

Level of the soul: *Rua'h*

See Sephira, Partsuf

יסודות

Yesodot

Plural of Yesod

See Yesod

יעקב

Ya'acov

Partsuf Ya'acov

Partsuf (configuration) *Ya'acov* is a masculine *Partsuf* to the left of *Partsuf Z"A.*

His *Keter* is at the level of *Tiferet* of *Partsuf Z"A,* and he extends until *Sephira Malkhut* of *Partsuf Z"A.*

There are different *Zivugim* (union) *between Partsuf Ya'acov and*

119

the feminine *(Ra'hel, Leah)* during the *Tefilot*:

Sha'hrit - *Ya'acov* and *Ra'hel*

Arvit – *Ya'acov* and *Leah* (from the chest up)

Tikun Hatsot – *Ya'acov* and *Leah* (from the chest down)

See Partsuf, Zivug

יצירה

Yetsirah

World of formation – of the angels

From the first configuration of *Adam Kadmon,* four worlds unfolded.

The third world to unfold is called *Yetsirah*; the world of formation, the world of the angels. It is under *Atsilut* and *Beriah* and on top of *'Asiah*.

It consists of five main *Partsufim: Arikh Anpin, Abah, Imah, Zeir Anpin* and *Nukvah*. One more *Partsuf, 'Atik Yomin,* is on top of them.

There is a screen (divider) that separates one world from another. From this screen, the ten *Sephirot* of the lower world come out from the ten *Sephirot* of the higher world. The three superior worlds of *Atsilut, Beriah* and *Yetsirah,* are interior to the fourth world of *'Asiah*.

In parallel to the four worlds *(ABYA),* there are four types of existence in our world; mineral corresponding to *'Asiah (action),* vegetal corresponding to *Yetsirah (formation),* animal corresponding to *Beriah (creation),* and man corresponding to *Atsilut (emanation).*

The world of *Yetsirah* is of the aspect of *MaH (45).* Thus, *Yetsirah* is of the aspect of *Partsuf Z"A.*

יצר

Yetser

Instinct – Impulse

The *Yetser Hatov* corresponds to the good or positive impulse in man, the *Yetser Hara'* is his bad or negative impulse.

The good deeds of man have an effect on the four higher worlds, his bad deeds; on the four lower worlds. It is only when man sins, that the negative side can grow in strength. The negative aspect grows inside him; this is his *Yetser Hara',* it cuts him off from the higher worlds, and uproots him from the *Kedushah.*

The *Yetser Hara'* almost constantly tries to seduce him, and make him stumble, while the *Yetser Hatov,* on the other side, tries to attract him to *Torah* and *Mitsvot* and to help him do the *Tikun* (rectification) of his *Neshama.*

The two aspects of *Yetser Tov* and *Yetser Hara'* are necessary for the guidance of justice, and to give man the possibility of free choice.

ירושלים

Yerushalaim

Jerusalem

The closest place to G-od's emanations.

ירידה

Yeridah

Descent

Because of the breaking of the vessels, there was a descent of all the worlds. The seven lower *Sephirot* of the world of *Atsilut* fell in the higher parts of *Beriah,* which became the *Atsilut* of today, *Beriah* fell in the higher part of *Yetsirah,* which became the *Beriah* of today, *Yetsirah* in the higher parts of *'Asiah,* which became the *Yetsirah* of today, *'Asiah* fell even lower and became the *'Asiah* of today.

See Zivug, Tikun, Shvirat HaKelim

יש מאין

Yesh Meein

Creation from nothing

There is a special force called "*Tsu'r T'K*", which has the power to create separate entities from nothing.

This force is not related to the *Sephirot*. It was first explained in the "*Sepher HaYetsrira*", which is the oldest Kabbalistic writing. It is only after being created that the guidance is taken over by the *Sephirot*.

ישסו"ת

ISOT

Partsufim Israel Saba and Tevunah

Initials

ישסו"ת ב

ISOT 2

Second Partsufim of Israel Saba and Tevunah

Initials

ישר

Yashar

Direct – Straight – Linear

See Or Yashar

ישראל

Israel

Partsuf Israel

All of Partsuf Zeir Anpin is called *Israel,* or sometimes only its top part.

ישראל

Israel

The land of Israel corresponds to *Partsuf (configuration) Nukvah – Ra'hel,* and is the closest to G-od's emanations.

ישראל סבא א

Israel Saba 1

Partsuf Israel Saba

Malkhut of *Partsuf Abah* is sometimes an independent *Partsuf.*
See Partsufim Israel Saba and Tevunah

ישראל סבא ב

Israel Saba 2

Partsuf Israel Saba 2

Malkhut of *Israel Saba* is sometimes an independent *Partsuf.*
See Partsufim Israel Saba and Tevunah, ISOT

ישראל סבא ותבונה

Israel Saba Ve Tevunah

Partsufim Israel Saba and Tevunah

The *Sephirot Malkhuts* of *Partsuf Abah* and *Imah* become distinct *Partsufim (configurations)*: *Israel Saba* and *Tevunah.* Their role is to be the *Mo'hin* (brains) of *Partsuf Z"A.*

They are also called by their initials *ISOT* or *ISOT* 2. The first *ISOT* are *Israel Saba and Tevunah,* the second *ISOT* are *Israel Saba 2* and *Tevunah 2.*

ISOT start from the *Sephira Tiferet* of *Abah* and *Imah* and extend downward.

The *Mo'hin* (brains) of *Z"A* are given to him by the *Zivug* (union) of *Abah* and *Imah.* Depending on the state of growth of *Z"A,* they are from *ISOT,* or directly from *Abah* and *Imah.*

כוונה

Kavanah

Intention – Concentration

There are different levels of *Kavanah*. The basic *Kavanah* is to understand the words, and concentrate on the intention of the blessing or the *Tefilah* (prayer). The higher level is to meditate on the different systems of permutation of names and *Partsufim* (configurations), to get a particular action or result.

The order of the *Tefilot* is based on the systems of ascension of the worlds as explained in the Kabbalah. At this level, we understand that our *Tefilot* have a direct influence on the superior worlds and on their guidance.

Starting from the first act in the morning of *Netilat Yadayim* (washing of the hands three times in alternation), until the end of the *Tefilah*, there is a constant elevation and adhesion of the worlds of *'Asiah, Yetsirah* and *Beriah* to *Atsilut.*

When saying a blessing with the Kabbalistic meditation on the appropriate words or names, we act and participate directly on the *Tikun* of the action or thing being blessed.

The *Hekhalot* (portals) are the different levels of ascension of the *Tefilot* before reaching the seventh highest *Hekhal (portal)*, *Kodesh Hakodashim*. Their principal function is to allow the adhesion and attachment, in various and particular ways during the *Tefilot*, until the *'Olam Atsilut* (during the *'Amidah*).

During the *Tefilot*, he who knows the system of ascension of the *Hekhalot* (portals), concentrates on the words where are hinted the precise action of the *Hekhal (portal)*. He aims to help in the realization of the particular *Zivug* (union) of the *Tefilah*.

When one understands the systems and actions of the *Tefilot*, he realizes the importance of our rituals, because only man, by praying and the accomplishment of the *Mitsvot,* can influence

these incredible forces.
See Tefilah

כוונות
Kavanot
Intentions – Concentration
See Kavanah

כולל
Kolel
One of the seven main types of *Gematriot*.
The *Ragil* value of the word + the numbers of letters.
Ex : הארץ   = 1106 + 4 = 1110
See Gematria

כח
Koa'h
Force – Strength
The different emanations of a particular light is dependent on the manifestations of the various levels of its force.

כחב
Ka'HaB
Keter, 'Hokhma, Binah
Initials

כיסא
Kisey
Throne
There are three main types of thrones:
Kisey HaDin - throne of justice
Kisey Hakavod - throne of glory
Kisey Ra'hamim - throne of mercy

125

כיסא הדין

Kisey HaDin

Throne of justice – rigor

From the throne of justice, the guidance is from the left pillar –
the pillar of rigor.

כיסא הכבו

Kisey HaKavod

Throne of glory

"In the presence of G-od"

כיסא הרחמים

Kisey Ra'hamim

Throne of mercy

From the throne of mercy, the guidance is from the middle pillar –
the pillar of mercy.

כלי

Keli

Recipient –Vessel

The light of G-od is unique and of equal force and quality. A
Sephira is in a way a "filter" which transforms this light in a
particular force or attribute, by which the Creator guides the
worlds.

Each *Sephira* is composed of a vessel called *Keli*, which holds its
part of light called *Or*. There is no difference in the *Or* itself, the
difference comes from the particularity, or position of the *Sephira*.

A *Partsuf* (configuration), as a *Sephira*, includes three
components: *Keli*, sparks, and light. The *Keli* is the recipient of
the light inside the *Sephira*.

The *Keli* has three levels: Interior, intermediate and exterior and
each one of these levels has particular actions and functions.

כלי חיצון

Keli 'Hitson

Exterior recipient - vessel

The level of *NHY* (Netsa'h, Hod, Yesod) of the *Keli* are its exterior aspect.

כלי פנימי

Keli Pnimi

Interior Keli

The level of *HBD* ('Hokhma, Binah, Da'at) of the *Keli* are its interior aspect.

כלי תיכון

Keli Tikhon

Intermediate Keli

The level of *HGT* ('Hesed, Gevurah, Tiferet) of the *Keli* are its intermediate aspect.

כלים

Kelim

Recipients – Vessels

See *Keli*

כתבי הארי

Kitve HaAri

Writings of the Ari

See *Ari Z'al*

כתר

Keter

Sephira – Crown

First and most important of the *Sephirot*.

Quality: Complete kindness to all, even to the not deserving.

Column: Center – *Ra'hamim* (mercy)

Position: Top – center

Other *Sephirot* on the same column: *Tiferet, Yesod, Malkhut.*

Partsufim made from this *Sephira:*

- *'Atik Yomin* and his *Nukvah*

- Arikh Anpin and his Nukvah

Corresponding name: *AHY-H* - אהי-ה

Corresponding *Miluy* (spelling) of name: *'A"V* - עב (72)

Corresponding vowel: *Kamatz*

Physical correspondence: Head

Level of the soul: *Ye'hidah*
See Sephira, Partsuf

כתר, חכמה, בינה
Keter, 'Hokhma, Binah

The three first *Sephirot*, often referred as the *Ga'R; Shalosh Rishonot* (the three first ones).

The roots of all the created are in the seven lower *Sephirot* (*Za"T*), the three first *Sephirot* are like a crown on the *Za"T* to repair and direct them. In the three first *Sephirot* there is not really a notion of damage, they are above men's deeds, and are not affected by their sins.

In the *Shvirat HaKelim* (breaking of the vessels)*,* the inferior part of *'Hokhma* and *Binah* did not contain their lights, they fell but did not break. These lower parts correspond to what is needed for the guidance of the seven lower *Sephirot*, if it had contained their lights, these *Sephirot* would not have broken, and the notions of *Kilkul* (damage) and *Tikun* (repair) not existed.
See Mo'hin.

ל"ב נתיבות חכמה

Lamed Bet Netivot 'Hokhma

32 Paths of wisdom

Thirty two paths of lights from the *Sephira 'Hokhma*. They are the twenty two letters plus the ten *Sephirot*. In the *Parasha Bereshit* the name of *Elokim* in mentioned 32 times.

לאה

Leah

Leah - Partsuf Nukvah

The *Partsuf Nukvah*, which represents the feminine – the principle of receiving, comprises of two distinct *Partsufim* (configurations): *Ra'hel* and *Leah*. *Partsuf Ra'hel* is of the aspect of kindness, *Partsuf Leah* of the aspect of rigor.

Partsuf Leah is on top of *Partsuf Ra'hel,* at the level of the *Sephira Da'at* of *Partsuf Z"A* and extends down to half of his *Tiferet*.

All the abundance that comes down to the world, proceeds from the various *Zivugim* (unions) of *Z"uN (Z"A* and *Nukvah)*.

There are five different *Zivugim*: Two with *Ra'hel* and three with *Leah*. The *Zivugim* with *Ra'hel* are of a higher level; being of the aspect of kindness, the ones with *Leah* are more of the aspect of rigor.

In the *Tefilah* (prayer) of *Min'ha*, there is the *Zivug* of *Israel* and *Leah*.

In the *Tefilah* of *'Arvit*, there is the *Zivug* of *Ya'acov* and *Leah* (from the chest up).

In *Tikun 'Hatsot*, there is the *Zivug* of *Ya'acov* and *Leah* (from the chest down).

See Malkhut, Nukvah, Zivug, Kavanah

לב

Lev

Heart

Usually identifies a center position or a main part.

לבוש

Levush

Garment

The *Levush (garment)* is an emanation given to a *Partsuf* to protect it from the negative forces.

The difference between the *Levush* and the encircling light is that the encircling light sustains the *Keli* (recipient), while the *Levush* is like a curtain that protects him.

There is also a *Levush* or envelope, which is necessary for the soul to attach to the body of man during his reincarnation (*Gilgul*). When another soul attaches to him (*'Ibur*), it could use the same *Levush (garment)* to remain in him.

לבנת הספיר

Livnat Hasapir

Name of a *Hekhal (portal)*.

First of seven *Hekhalot*, corresponding to *Sephira Yesod* and *Malkhut*.

The *Hekhalot* are the different levels of ascension of the *Tefilot* (prayers) before reaching the final seventh *Hekhal* (portal); *Kodesh Hakodashim*.

להאיר

Lehair

Illuminate

A *Sephira* can "illuminate" or transmit its light to another *Sephira* or *Partsuf*.

להחיות

LeHa'hayot

To Live – Sustain

After the *Shvirat HaKelim (breaking of the vessels)*, the *Kelim* fell to the lower worlds. To sustain them after they broke, 288 sparks of the lights came down as well. A connection with their own original lights was needed to keep them alive.

For their livelihood, the negative forces get strength by attaching to the exteriority of the *Sephirot*; they nourish from their lights and gain more power to act negatively.

All and everything is sustained by one and only one source; the light of G-od, which is bestowed through the *Partsufim* and *Sephirot*.

להחמיר

LeHa'hmir

To be more stringent

A strict observance of all the details when accomplishing a *Mitsva* or *Tefilah*.

להנהיג

LeHanhig

To guide

See Hanhagah

לוצאטו

Luzzatto

Rabbi Moshe 'Haim Luzzatto – Ram'hal

Born in Padua, Italy in 1707, died in Israel in 1746.

From an early age, Rabbi Moshe 'Haim Luzzatto showed an exceptional talent for the study of Kabbalah, it is said that when he was only fourteen, he already knew all the Kabbalah of the Ari Z'al by heart, and nobody knew about it, not even his parents. He was a very prolific writer and wrote on the all aspects of the Torah and the Kabbalah. Some of his main works are "Kala'h Pit'he'Hokhma" "Klalut Hallan" "Adir Bamaron".

ליאדי
Liadi
Rabbi Shneur Zalman of Liadi – The Alter Rebbe
Born in Russia, 1745, died in Russia in 1813.
The "Baal HaTanya", founder of the 'Habad -
Lubavitch movement. He was a descendant of the Maharal of Prague. He studied under the Maggid of Mezritch the writings of the Ari and composed the "Tanya".

לידה
Leida
Birth
All the *Tikunim* (rectification) of the *Partsufim* (masculine and feminine) are achieved by way of *Zivug* (union), gestation and birth. When a *Partsuf* (configuration) is complete and arranged, it is revealed, this is called its birth (*Leida*).
There is afterwards a period called suckling, and finally the growth, so that the *Partsuf* will be fully independent.

למטה
Lemata
To lower
A process of descent.

למעלה
Lema'la
To higher
A process of ascent.

לפרקים

Lifrakim

Intermittently

Some actions or illuminations are occasional. The *Zivug* (union) of *Partsuf Abah* and *Imah i*s constant, but the one of *Partsuf ISOT* is occasional. The *Zivug* of *Abah* and *Imah* for the liveliness of the worlds is constant, but the one for the *Mo'hin* (brains) is occasional.

לקבל

Lekabel

To receive

The word Kabbalah comes from the verb *Lekabel* (to receive), but to receive it is first necessary to want, and to become a *Keli* (recipient) able to receive and contain this knowledge. A *Kabbalist* is a person that is accepted to receive this knowledge, and is able to hold it by living in the path of *Torah* and rightness to strengthen himself constantly.

When one decides that he wants to know his Creator, in learning this science he realizes his smallness compared to these incredible forces, the perfection of the Lord and His infinite love for His creatures.

Since the intention of the Creator is to bestow goodness on His creatures, all the levels of creation were put in place so His kindness could emanate to them, yet in such a way that they would be able to receive it.

The *Ein Sof* (infinite), *B'H* influences when there is instigation from the receiver. This influence is transmitted by different illuminations (*Sephirot*), and then by *Nukvah* after her *Zivug* (union) with *Z"A,* to the receiver (man).

See Kabbalah

מ"ב
MaV

MaV (42)
Name of 42 letters made by the four letters of the name
י-ה-ו-ה, the *Miluy* (spelling) of each one of the four letters for a
total of ten letters, and the *Miluy* of each one of these ten letters
for a total of twenty eight.
This name is hinted in the recital of the *Kadish* during the *Tefilah*
(prayer). It makes possible the ascent of each world to the next
higher world.

מ"ד
M"D

Mayin Dukhrin (masculine waters)
Initials

מ"ה
MaH (45)

Miluy (spelling) of the name י-ה-ו-ה with a total of 45
The creative forces or energies are the different powers in the
four letters of the name of G-od י-ה-ו-ה, and the various letters
added to make their different spellings. Depending on which
letters are used, the numerical value of the name changes, and
each one of these possibilities becomes different in its nature and
actions.

The four *Miluyim* (spellings) are:
- עב, סג , מה, בן -
- *'A"V* (72), *SaG* (63), *MaH* (45), *BaN* (52)

עב – יוד הי ויו הי   - *'A"V* = 72
סג – יוד הי ואו הי   - *SaG* = 63

יוד הא ואו הא - מה - *MaH* = 45
יוד הה וו הה – בן - *BaN* = 52

Each name can also be divided and subdivided as:
'A"V of 'A"V, SaG of 'A"V, MaH of 'A"V ...
BaN of BaN of SaG, SaG of MaH of 'A"V etc.

The name of *MaH* (45) is the *Miluyim* (spelling) of א, which is a (ו) (Vav) line in the middle (mercy) that unites two ' (Yud) (kindness and rigor). It is of a masculine aspect and represents mercy.

יוד הא ואו הא - מה - *MaH* = 45

After the breaking of the *Kelim* (recipients) and the separation from their lights, it was necessary for the guidance of the world that reparation be done. From the forehead of *Adam Kadmon* came out ten *Sephirot* of the aspect of the name of *MaH* (45); corresponding to the masculine - reparation. In contrast, the *Sephirot* of *BaN* (52) correspond to the feminine aspect - rigor, and are the root of deterioration. The *Tikun (reparation)* was the union of *MaH* and *BaN* in complex arrangements, as to allow the feminine *BaN* to be repaired by the masculine *MaH* and for the *Sephirot* to stand in the three-column arrangement of kindness, rigor and mercy

See Orot HaMetsa'h, Sephirot Shel MaH

מ"ן
M"N
Mayin Nukvin (feminine waters)
Initials

מאציל

Maatsil

Emanator

His light, force or energy is without end, and of such holiness and intensity, that it is not possible for any being to exist in its proximity.

His first act in this creation was then to set limits to His light, so that it would not emanate with its full force.

Since the intention of the Creator is to bestow goodness on His creatures, all the levels of creation were put in place so His kindness could emanate to them, yet in such a way that they would be able to receive it.

The *Sephirot* are the links between the Emanator and the guidance of the world. By them, are manifested the actions of the *Ein Sof*, - the Emanator to the receivers.

His emanations are transmitted by different illuminations of the aspect of *MaH (45)*, and then by *Nukvah* after her *Zivug* with *Partsuf Z"A*.

מגיד

Maggid

Celestial mentor

A *Maggid* reveals himself to teach celestial secrets.

The Ram'hal had the revelation of a *Maggid*, under his dictation he wrote thousands of pages and revealed magnificent secrets.

מדבר

Medaber

Speaking

In parallel to the four worlds of *Atsilut, Beriah, Yetsirah* and *'Asiah,* there are four types of existence in our world: mineral (דומם), vegetal (צומח), animal (חי), and the speaking (מדבר)..

Mineral corresponding to 'Asiah, vegetal corresponding to Yetsirah, animal corresponding to Beriah, and the speaking corresponding to Atsilut.

מדה

Midah

Attribute - Quality – Measure

The light of G-od is unique, of equal force, quality and beyond all description. Since the concept of limitlessness is above our human comprehension, we therefore have to use terms accessible to our understanding. In Kabbalah the term 'quality' is used, to differentiate the various transformations of this "simple light", and to help us understand its effects upon the guidance of the worlds.

The Sephirot or Partsufim are called the attributes or qualities of G-od. A Sephira is in a way a "filter" which transforms this light in a particular force or quality, by which the Creator guides the worlds.

See Sephirot, Partsufim

מדרגה

Madregah

Level

A level of importance.

The actions or manifestations of the lights and emanations depend on their level of importance.

מדת הדין

Midat HaDin

The attribute (quality) of judgment

The light of G-od is unique, of equal force, quality and beyond all description. In Kabbalah the term 'quality' is used, to differentiate the various transformations of this "unique light", and to help us understand its effects upon the guidance of the worlds.

The *Sephirot* or *Partsufim* (configurations) are called the attributes or qualities of G-od. A *Sephira* is in a way a "filter" which transforms this light in a particular force or quality, by which the Creator guides the worlds. One of these manifestations of this light once filtered by the *Sephira Gevurah* emanates rigor.

The *Sephirot* are arranged in three columns: right, left and middle, representing the guidance of the world in the manner of *'Hesed*, *Din* and *Ra'hamim* - Kindness, rigor and mercy. In the attribute of rigor, the guidance is from the left pillar – the pillar of rigor, it contains the *Sephirot*: *Binah*, *Gevurah*, *Hod*. The corresponding name to this attribute is: *Elohi-m* - אלהי-ם

Some *Partsufim* are masculine and bestow kindness, others are feminine and bestow rigor. By their union, different equilibriums of these two forces (Kindness and rigor), make the guidance. Complete rigor will be the destruction of anything not perfect, while complete kindness will permit everything without restriction. Thus we see that everything that is, and happens, is always composed of a variable measure and balance of these two forces.

Rigor is mostly manifested by all the feminine aspects as: the name of *BaN (52)*, the *Sephira Gevurah* and by all the concealments of the masculine aspects which represent bounty.

There are particular moments, or days of rigor during the year. This is dependent on the different position of the *Partsufim*. In the absence of *Zivug* (union) when the masculine and feminine *Partsuf* are back to back, it corresponds to dissimulation and rigor.

מדת החסד

Midat Ha'Hesed

The attribute of (quality) bounty

The light of G-od is unique, of equal force, quality and beyond all description. In Kabbalah the term 'quality' is used, to differentiate the various transformations of this "unique light", and to help us understand its effects upon the guidance of the worlds.

The *Sephirot* or *Partsufim* are called the attributes or qualities of G-od. A *Sephira* is in a way a "filter" which transforms this light in a particular force or quality, by which the Creator guides the worlds.

The linear *Sephirot* are arranged in three columns: right, left and middle, representing the guidance of the world in the manner of *'Hesed*, *Din* and *Ra'hamim* - Kindness, rigor and mercy. Some *Partsufim* are masculine and bestow kindness, others are feminine and bestow rigor. By their union, different equilibriums of the two forces of Kindness and rigor make the guidance. When the masculine and feminine *Partsuf* are face to face it is the ideal level and corresponds to the bestowing of abundance.

In the attribute of bounty, the guidance is from the right pillar – the pillar of kindness.

The corresponding name to this attribute is:

YHV-K -יה-ו-ה-י

See Sephirot, Partsufim

מדת הרחמים

Midat HaRa'hamim

The attribute of (quality) Mercy

The light of G-od is unique, of equal force, quality and beyond all description. In Kabbalah the term 'quality' is used, to differentiate the various transformations of this "unique light", and to help us understand its effects upon the guidance of the worlds.

The *Sephirot* or *Partsufim* are called the attributes or qualities of G-od. A *Sephira* is in a way a "filter" which transforms this light in a particular force or quality, by which the Creator guides the worlds.

The linear *Sephirot* are arranged in three columns: right, left and middle, representing the guidance of the world in the manner of *'Hesed, Din* and *Ra'hamim* - Kindness, rigor and mercy. Some *Partsufim* are masculine and bestow kindness, others are feminine and bestow rigor. By their union, different equilibriums of the two forces of Kindness and rigor make the guidance.

In the attribute of mercy the guidance is from the middle pillar – the pillar of *Ra'hamim*. This Guidance makes the balance between the guidance of rigor and bounty.

See Sephirot, Partsufim

מהות
Mahut
Essence
Nature or inner quality.

מוח
Moa'h
Brain
See Mo'hin

מוחא סתימאה
Mo'ha Stimaah
Third of the three heads of Arikh Anpin
The three heads of *Arikh Anpin* are the roots of the direction of kindness, rigor and mercy. They emanate from *Arikh Anpin* to *Abah* and *Imah,* and from there, to the *Mo'hin* (brains) of *Z"A*.
The third head is *Mo'ha* - It is the *Sephira 'Hokhma* of *Arikh*.

מוחין

Mo'hin

Brains

The *Mo'hin* are the directive force given to the *Partsuf* (configuration). There are interior and encircling *Mo'hin*. The interior *Mo'hin* are the *Sephirot NHY* (Netsa'h, Hod, Yesod) of the superior *Partsuf* that enter inside the lower *Partsuf* to be his brains or intelligence. The encircling *Mo'hin* stand on the outside.

There are two distinct *Mo'hin* that come to *Z"A*: *Mo'hin* of *Imah* arrive first, and then the *Mo'hin* of *Abah*. The *Mo'hin* that are given from *Abah* and *Imah* to *Z"A*, are called his (צלמ) *Tselem* and do not enter completely in him; only the *NHY* (Netsa'h, Hod, Yesod) do, the rest stays on top of him, encircling his head.

There are two gestations and two growths for *Partsuf Z"A*. The *Mo'hin* of the first growth are from *Tevunah*, the *Mo'hin* of the second growth are from *Imah*. It is only after the second growth, that *Z"A* has reached its full potential. This is *Gadlut* 2.

See Partsuf, Gadlut

מוחין דגדלות

Mo'hin of Gadlut

Brains of growth

There are *Mo'hin* (brains) of *Gadlut* 1 and *Mo'hin* of *Gadlut* 2.

When *Partsuf Z"A* receives all his *Mo'hin*; interior and encircling (*Tselem*) from *Tevunah*, they are *Mo'hin* of *Gadlut* 1. When he receives all his *Mo'hin* directly from *Imah*, they are *Mo'hin* of *Gadlut* 2 and he has now attained his full growth.

See Partsuf, Gadlut

מוחין דקתנות

Mo'hin of Katnut

Brains of infancy

There are *Mo'hin* (brains) of *Katnut* 1 and *Mo'hin* of *Katnut* 2.
When *Partsuf Z"A* only receives the *NHY (Netsa'h, Hod, Yesod)* of his *Mo'hin* - the interior, but not the encircling (*Tselem*), from *Tevunah;* they are the *Mo'hin* of *Katnut* 1.
When he receives the *NHY (Netsa'h, Hod, Yesod)* of his *Mo'hin* directly from *Imah,* they are the *Mo'hin* of *Katnut* 2.
See Partsuf, Gadlut

מוחין מקיפין
Mo'hin Makifin
Encircling Brains
The encircling *Mo'hin* are of a higher aspect than the interior *Mo'hin*. They do not enter inside the lower *Partsuf*, and encircle him on the outside. It is the encircling - למ of the of the complete *Mo'hin* - צלמ
See Mo'hin

מוחין פנימין
Mo'hin Penimim
Interior Brains
The interior *Mo'hin* enter inside the lower *Partsuf*. It is the *NHY (Netsa'h, Hod, Yesod)* of the superior *Partsuf* which are composed of nine parts, and correspond to the צ. They spread in the nine *Sephirot* of *Z"A*.
See Mo'hin

מושך
Moshekh
Attracts – Draws
A light or emanation attracts or draws another for the purpose of *Tikun* or *Zivug*.

מזון

Mazon

Food – Subsistence

For their sustenance the negative forces get strength by attaching to the exteriority of the *Sephirot*.

מזל

Mazal

Luck - Destiny – Constellation

Each day and moment is of a different emanation. These emanations vary in their positivity or negativity.

The seven main planets correspond to seven *Sephirot*.

Planet		Sephira
Moon	לבנה	'Hesed
Mars	מאדים	Gevurah
Sun	חמה	Tiferet
Venus	נוגה	Netsa'h
Mercury	כוכב	Hod
Saturn	שבתאי	Yesod
Jupiter	צדק	Malkhut

מזל נוצר

Mazal Notser

There are hairs (lights) that come out from the face of *Sephira* '*Hokhma Stimaah* of *Partsuf Arikh Anpin* and spread downward. They divide in thirteen, and are called the thirteen *Tikunim* (rectifications) of the *Dikna* (beard) of *Arikh Anpin*.

Mazal Notser is the eighth Tikun of the Dikna of Arikh Anpin, corresponding to (the beard on) The upper chin.

See Sheta'h 'Elyon

מזל נקה
Mazal Nakeh
There are hairs (lights) that come out from the face *Sephira*
'Hokhma Stimaah of *Partsuf Arikh Anpin,* and spread downward.
They divide in thirteen, and are called the thirteen *Tikunim* of the
Dikna (beard) of *Arikh Anpin.*
*Mazal Nake is the thirteen Tikun of the Dikna of Arikh Anpin,
corresponding to* (the beard under) The lower chin
See Sheta'h Ta'hton

מחשבה
Ma'hashavah
Thought
Intention, will.
"There are many thoughts in a man's heart, but it is the counsel
of G-od that will stand" (Mishle – Proverbs 19, 21)

מטה
Matah
Lower
In general, lower refers to inferior or less important.

מטה האלהים
Mateh Elokim
Scepter of Elokim
Diagonal light or *Partsuf* on the left side of *Leah.*
This light, or *Partsuf*, is not considered as a complete *Partsuf*; its
actions are temporary and at particular times only.

מטה משה
Mateh Moshe
Scepter of Moshe
Diagonal light or *Partsuf* on the right side of *Leah.*

This light, or *Partsuf*, is not considered as a complete *Partsuf*; its actions are temporary and at particular times only

מטטרו"ן
Matatro"n
Name of one of the three great princes of the Angels.

מידות
Midot
Attributes – Qualities
See Midah

מיין
Mayin
Water
Emanations allegorically called masculine or feminine waters.
See Mayin Dukhrin, Mayin Nukvin

מיין דוכרין
Mayin Dukhrin
Masculine waters
One of two emanations allegorically called masculine or feminine waters.

The *Tikun* (rectification) is done by the *Zivug* (union) of the masculine and the feminine. There are two conditions needed for the *Zivug* to be possible: the *Partsufim* (configurations) have to be constructed, and the feminine has to stimulate a reaction from the masculine. This stimulation happens when the *Partsuf Nukvah* brings up her *Mayin Nukvin* (feminine waters) of the feminine aspect of *BaN* (52), which then provoke the descent of the *Mayin Dukhrin* from the masculine aspect of *MaH* (45).

The masculine reacts, stimulated by the feminine, which is in turn motivated by the actions of man. In addition, because of the

Tikunim (rectifications) realized by men with the Tefilot and the Mitsvot, Nukvah brings up her Mayin Nukvin, and in response; Mayin Dukhrin come down for the completion of the Zivug.

Mayin Dukhrin and Mayin Nukvin are the essential of the Zivug. Mayin Nukvin proceeds from the feminine and Mayin Dukhrin from the masculine. There is no Mayin Dukhrin without Mayin Nukvin, and there is no Mayin Nukvin without desire.

מיין נוקבין
Mayin Nukvin
Feminine waters
One of two emanations allegorically called masculine or feminine waters.

The Tikun (rectification) is done by the Zivug (union) of the masculine and the feminine. There are two conditions needed for the Zivug to be possible: the Partsufim (configurations) have to be constructed, and the feminine has to stimulate a reaction from the masculine. This stimulation happens when the Partsuf Nukvah brings up her Mayin Nukvin (feminine waters) of the feminine aspect of BaN (52), which then provoke the descent of the Mayin Dukhrin from the masculine aspect of MaH (45).

The masculine reacts, stimulated by the feminine, which is in turn motivated by the actions of man. In addition, because of the Tikunim (rectifications) realized by men with the Tefilot and the Mitsvot, Nukvah brings up her Mayin Nukvin, and in response; Mayin Dukhrin come down for the completion of the Zivug.

Mayin Dukhrin and Mayin Nukvin are the essential of the Zivug. Mayin Nukvin proceeds from the feminine and Mayin Dukhrin from the masculine. There is no Mayin Dukhrin without Mayin Nukvin, and there is no Mayin Nukvin without desire.

See Zivug, Malkhut, Nukvah

מילוי

Miluy

Spelling

The creative forces or energies are the different powers in the four letters of the name of G-od י-ה-ו-ה, and the various letters added to make their different spellings. Depending on which letters are used, the numerical value of the name changes, and each one of these possibilities becomes different in its nature and actions.

The letters that are added for the different spellings of the letters are: י ה ו א ד

The different spellings of the letters are:

The letter י *(Yud)* can only be spelled one way: יוד

The letter ה *(He)* can be spelled with a י *(Yud)* or an א *(Aleph)* or a ה *(He)*: הא הה הי

The Letter ו *(Vav)* can be spelled with a יו *(Yud and Vav)* or with או *(Aleph and Vav)* or

With a ו *(Vav)*: ואו ויו וו

The four *Miluyim* (spellings) are:

עב ,סג , מה, בן - *'A"V, SaG, MaH, BaN* -

יוד הי ויו הי – עב   - *'A"V* = 72

יוד הי ואו הי – סג   - *SaG* = 63

יוד הא ואו הא - מה   - *MaH* = 45

יוד הה וו הה – בן   - *BaN* = 52

Each name can also be divided and subdivided as:

'A"V of 'A"V, SaG of 'A"V, MaH of 'A"V …

BaN of BaN of SaG, SaG of MaH of 'A"V etc.

The name of *'A"V* is of the highest level of the four names. Its *Miluy* is with the letter י (*Yud*) for a total of 72.

The name of *SaG* is the second level of the four names. Its *Miluy* is with the letter י (*Yud*) and א (*Aleph*) for a total of 63.

The name of *MaH* (45) is the third level of the four names. Its *Miluy* is with the letter א (*Aleph*) for a total of 45.

The name of *BaN* (52) is the fourth level of the four names. Its *Miluy* is with the letter ו (*Vav*) for a total of 52.

All the emanations and *Sephirot* that came out of *Adam Kadmon* (*Primordial man*) by way of his apertures were of the various aspects of these four names. They have different actions and *Tikunim*, and all the *Partsufim (configurations)* will be constructed by their union.

See 'Av, SaG, MaH, BaN

מילוי גמטריות
Miluy of Gematriot

One of the seven main types of *Gematriot*.
The sum of the spelling of each letter.

Letter	Miluy	Value
ה	הא	6
א	אלף	111
ר	ריש	510
צ	צדי	104

Ex : הארץ = 731

See Gematria

מילויים
Miluyim
Spellings

See Miluy

מיעוט

Mi'ut

Decrease – Diminution

There is a decrease or diminution of an emanation depending on its stage of evolution.

מיתוק

Mituk

Sweetening – Mitigation

A mitigation or sweetening of the *Gevurot* (rigors) occurs when they are in direct contact with the *'Hasadim* (kindnesses).

See 'Hasadim, Gevurot

מלאך

Malakh

Angel

See Malakhim

מלאכים

Malakhim

Angels

The world of the angels is the third world; *'Olam Yetsirah* - the world of formation.

The angels of peace make ten groups and serve the ten *Sephirot* of the right, while the angels of destruction make ten levels and serve the ten *Sephirot* from the lower opposite side.

There are two types of angels: the angels of the nature who were created at the beginning of the world, they are in charge of the nature itself. The second type are the angels of "reward and punishment". They accomplish the will of the divine light inside the *Sephirot,* and are renewed constantly depending on the deeds of men.

The ten groups of positive angels are divided as follows: three groups in the world of *Beriah* (creation*)*, six groups in the world of *Yetsirah* (formation)*,* and one group in the world of *'Asiah* (action).

The princes of these three groups are: *Shemu'i-El, Matatro-n, Vihu-El.* They are also divided in four camps: Michael, Gabriel, Ouriel, and Rephael.

The name of the angels and the princes of the ten groups are:

Group	Angels	Prince
1	שרפי-ם Seraphi-m	יהו-אל Yehu-El
2	אופני-ם Ofani-m	רפ-אל Repha-El
3	כרובי-ם Keruvi-m	כרו-ב Keru-v
4	שנאני-ם Shanani-m	צדקי-אל Tsadiki-El
5	תרשישי-ם Tarshishi-m	תרשי-ש Tarshi-sh
6	חשמלי-ם 'Hashmali-m	חשמ-ל 'Hashm-al
7	מלאכי-ם Malakhi-m	עוזי-אל 'uzi-El
8	בני אלהי-ם Bene Eloh-im	חפני-אל 'Hafni-El
9	אישי-ם Ishi-m	צפני-ה Tsefani-ah
10	אראלי-ם Areli-m	מיכ-אל Mikha-El

The other entity, which is called the *Sitra A'hra* – (the other side, or the negative force) has its own four worlds of *Atsilut, Beriah, Yetsirah* and *'Asiah,* it also has *Partsufim, Sephirot, Hekhalot* and angels, as in the positive world, but of a lower force. Its destructive angels subdivide in the same order as well, depending on their importance they are from its own worlds of *Beriah, Yetsirah* or *'Asiah.*

מלך
Melekh
King
See Malkin

מלכות
Malkhut
Sephira (Royalty)
Tenth of the *Sephirot.*
Quality: Guidance that translates all the superior emanations into one that is reflected to the creation.
Link or connection between all the superior *Sephirot* and man.
Column: Center – *Ra'hamim* (mercy)
Position: Middle – Bottom
Other *Sephirot* on the same column: *Keter, Tiferet, Yesod*
Partsufim made from this *Sephira:*
Nukvah, divided in two *Partsufim: Ra'hel* and *Leah*
Corresponding name: *Adona-y* – אדנ-י
Corresponding *Miluy* (spelling) of name: *BaN* (52)- בן
Corresponding vowel: none
Physical correspondence: Crown on the masculine organ
Level of the soul: *Nefesh*
See Sephira, Partsuf, Nukvah

מלכין קדמאין

Malkin Kadmain

Kings of Edom – corresponding to Z'aT

The seven kings of Edom that died (Bereshit, 36, 31), correspond to
the seven lower *Sephirot* (*Z'aT*) that broke.

See Shvirat HaKelim

מן

Manna

Diagonal light or *Partsuf* (configuration) on the left side of *Partsuf*
Z"A.

This light, or *Partsuf*, is not considered as a complete *Partsuf*; its
actions are temporary and at particular times only

מנצפ"ך

MNTSP"KH

Five Gevurot

The five ending letters correspond to the five *Gevurot* (rigors).

See Gevurot, Mayin Nukvin

מעשה בראשית

Ma'ase Bereshit

Works or acts of the creation

Name given for all the details of the beginning of the creation,
from the *Tsimtsum*, the first worlds, the *Sephirot* etc.

מעשה המרקבה

Ma'ase Hamerkava

Works or acts of the Heavenly Chariot

Name given for all the details of the *Sephirot, Partsufim, Tikunim*
and *Zivugim* that make the guidance.

מצוה

Mitsva

Commandment

The Torah contains four levels of comprehension, of which the highest is the *Sod (secret)*. At this level, we understand that our *Tefilot* and the accomplishment of each one of the *Mitsvot,* has a direct influence on the superior worlds and on their guidance. The Kabbalah teaches us that the world is guided by an extremely complex system of forces or lights, which through their interactions, provoke chain reactions that impact directly on man and the worlds. Each one of these reactions has numerous ramifications, with many details and results. Only man, by praying and the accomplishment of the *Mitsvot,* can influence these incredible forces.

As there are 613 *Mitsvot,* there are 613 veins and bones to man, 613 parts to the soul, and each *Sephira* and *Partsuf* also has 613 parts. This number is not arbitrary as there are important interrelations and interactions between them.

After the *Shvirat HaKelim (breaking of the vessels)*, the goal of all the works, deeds and prayers of men in this existence, is to help and participate in the ascent of the fallen 288 sparks to their origin. This can be done by accomplishing the *Mitsvot* and the *Tefilot*. At the completion of this *Tikun* of unification between the fallen sparks and their *Kelim,* it will be the time of the resurrection of the dead and the arrival of *Moshia'h.*

The *Klipot* (husks) are the manifestation of the negative force, they obstruct the lights of the *Sephirot,* conceal man from his root, and from the light. Because of the bad deeds of the lower beings, the *Klipot* get their strength and do evil in the world by attaching to the higher lights. The *Tikunim* (rectifications) of the lower beings is to detach these *Klipot* from the *Kedushah* by accomplishing the *Mitsvot* and the *Tefilot*.

The *Tikun* of the soul is realized by the *Gilgul* (reincarnation), and by the *'Ibur* (attachment). By accomplishing what he did not accomplish of the 613 *Mitsvot*, man makes the necessary *Tikun* of his soul, which can now elevate to the higher realms, and rejoin its source.

See Tefilot, Kavanah

מצוות

Mitsvot

Commandments

See Mitsva

מצח הרצון

Metsa'h HaRatson

Forehead of mercy

The fourth *Tikun* (action) of the head of *Arikh Anpin* - רעוא דמצחא (*Ra'ava Demits'ha*) is realized by the *Sephira Yesod* of *Partsuf 'Atik*; his *'Hasadim* shine from the forehead of *Arikh Anpin*. When it is fully revealed, all the rigors are annulled.

מקבל

Mekabel

Receiver

Since the intention of the Creator is to bestow goodness on His creatures, all the levels of creation were put in place so His kindness could emanate to them, yet in such a way that they would be able to receive it.

The *Ein Sof*, *B'H* influences when there is instigation from the receiver, the latter corresponding to the aspect of *BaN* (52). This influence is transmitted by different illuminations (*Sephirot*), and then by *Partsuf* (configuration) *Nukvah* after her *Zivug* (union) with *Partsuf Z"A*, to the receiver (man).

For the *Sephirot* there are also interactions of influencer and receiver. The lower *Partsuf* is guided and receives his *Mo'hin* (brains) from the higher *Partsuf*.

מקובל

Mekubal

Kabbalist - Accepted

The word Kabbalah comes from the verb *Lekabel* (to receive), but to receive it is first necessary to be prepared, and to be a *Keli (recipient)* able to receive and contain this knowledge.

A *Mekubal* is a person who is accepted to receive this knowledge, and is able to hold it by living in the path of Torah and rightness to strengthen himself constantly.

מקום

Makom

Place – space

Until the world was created, He and His Name were One. He willed to create, and contracted His light to create all beings by giving them a space.

When His light retracted, forming the round space, a trace of it, called the *Reshimu,* remained inside. This lower intensity light, allowed a space (*Makom*) of existence, for all the created worlds and beings. By "space" (*Makom*), one should not understand a physical space, but rather a possibility of existence since there is no existence that does not have its own space.

Also one of the names of G-od.

מקור

Makor

Source – Origin

Each emanation has its source in the higher realms

מקיף
Makif
Encircling
See Or Makif

מקיפין
Makifin
Encircling
See Or Makif

מרקבה
Merkavah
Heavenly chariot
The *Partsufim* (configurations), *Sephirot* and the *Sephirot* tree, with all their inter-relations, actions and illuminations.

משובח
Meshuba'h
First rate – Important
The emanations that come from the higher lights are of a finer and stronger force.

משל
Mashal
Allegory
Sometimes used to explain or illustrate difficult concepts.

משפיע
Mashpia'h
Influencer
Since the intention of the Creator is to bestow goodness on His

creatures, all the levels of creation were put in place so His kindness could emanate to them, yet in such a way that they would be able to receive it.

The *Sephirot* are the links between the Emanator and the guidance of the world. By them, are manifested the influence of the *Ein Sof*, - the Influencer to the receivers.

His Influence is transmitted by different illuminations of the aspect of *MaH (45)*, and then by *Partsuf* (configuration) *Nukvah* after her *Zivug* (union) with *Partsuf Z"A.*

מתלבש

Mitlabesh

Dress

Partsufim dress on, or in, each other. The more important *Partsuf* will dress inside the less important to direct him.

See Partsufim, Mo'hin

מתערין

Mit'arin

Awakening

See Eta'aruta de La'ila, Eta'aruta de Tata

מתקלא

Matkala

Since the intention of the Creator is to bestow goodness on His creatures, all the levels of creation were put in place so His kindness could emanate to them, yet in such a way that they would be able to receive it.

With the emanation of the lights of *MaH (45)* and *BaN (52)*, He could have done the *Tikun* (rectification) of all the worlds after the *Shvirat HaKelim (breaking of the vessels),* but then there would not have been a reason for the participation of man in this *Tikun.*

To give a possibility to man to act and repair the creation, G-od restrained in a way, his outflow of kindness to this world, and this is the role of the *Matkala*.

The *Matkala* is the root of all the *Tikunim* and has its origin in *Sephira 'Hesed* and *Gevurah* of the *Radl'a* (the unknown head).

See Radl'a

נאצל
Neetsal
Emanated being
Men, angels etc.

נביא
Navi
Prophet
The prophecy originates from the *Sephira Netsa'h* or the *Sephira Hod.* These *Sephirot* have three parts each. The difference between the levels of the prophets depends from which one of the three parts of these *Sephirot*, they receive the prophecy.

נגה
Nogah
Nogah - Glow
One of the four main levels of *Klipot* corresponding to the four lower worlds.
See Klipot

נהי
NeHY
Netsa'h, Hod and Yesod
Initials of the third triplet of the *Sephirot: Netsa'h, Hod and Yesod.* They mostly act together as the interior *Mo'hin* (brains) for a lower *Partsuf.*

נהר
Nahar
River – Stream
The outflows of some emanations are sometimes described as one or more streams or rivers.

נוגה
Nogah

Name of a *Hekhal (portal)*.

Third of seven *Hekhalot*, corresponding to *Netsa'h*.

The *Hekhalot* are the different levels of ascension of the *Tefilot* (prayers) before reaching the final seventh *Hekhal* (portal); *Kodesh Hakodashim*.

נוטריקון
Notrikun (acronym)

Notrikun is a method of interpretation in which initials of different words make a new word.

אל מלך נאמן = אמן

נוקבא
Nukvah

Feminine - Sephira Malkhut – Partsuf Ra'hel, Leah

The *Partsuf* (configuration) *Nukvah* represents the feminine – the principle of receiving. It comprises of two distinct *Partsufim*: *Ra'hel* and *Leah*.

The masculine *Partsuf Zeir Anpin* and the feminine *Nukvah*, are the root of all the created. It is by them, that the guidance is manifested.

There is perfection for the masculine only when it completes itself with its feminine, and there can be abundance only when the masculine and the feminine are in harmony. This abundance comes down to the world, by the various *Zivugim* (unions) of *Zeir Anpin* with *Nukvah*. The one of *Partsuf Israel* and *Partsuf Ra'hel* is of the highest level. *Israel* represents the essential of *Z"A*, and *Ra'hel* of *Nukvah*. The abundance that is bestowed by this *Zivug* is the most complete. The other *Zivugim* of *Zeir Anpin* and *Nukvah* are of different levels, in various times, and of lesser plenitude

There are two conditions needed for the *Zivug* (union) to be possible: the *Partsufim* have to be constructed, and the feminine has to stimulate a reaction from the masculine. This stimulation happens because of the *Tikunim* (rectifications) realized by men with the *Tefilot* (prayers) and *Mitsvot*. *Nukvah* brings up emanations called *Mayin Nukvin* (feminine waters of the aspect of *BaN* *(52)*), which then provokes the descent of emanations called *Mayin Dukhrin* (masculine waters of the aspect of *MaH* *(45)*) from the masculine, for the completion of the *Zivug*.

This is the goal of the service of the creatures; to help prepare the *Partsufim Z"A* and *Nukvah* for the *Zivug*, and this, by the elevation and adhesion of the worlds of *Beriah*, *Yetsirah* and *'Asiah* to the *Hekhalot* (portals) of *Nukvah* of the world of *Atsilut*, during the *Tefilot*.

The *Nukvah* (*Ra'hel*) also has an aspect of *Tefilin*, and attaches on the left arm (*Gevurah*) of *Z"A*. She has four *Parashiot* in her *Tefilin*, and receives her *Mo'hin* (brains) through the *Sephira Netsa'h* and *Hod* of *Partsuf Z"A*.

See Partsuf, Zivug, Tikun, Partsuf Z"A

נימין

Nimin

Extremities of the hairs on the head

From the *Partsuf* (configuration) *Arikh Anpin*, there are emanations that come out from its head to act and influence on the guidance called; the *Tikunim* (actions) of *Arikh Anpin*.

One of these *Tikunim* of *Arikh Anpin* is from *Avirah* (*Sephira Da'at* of *'Atik*; between *Sephira Keter* and *'Hokhma*) It is called נימין (*Nimin*); the extremities of the hairs on the head.

The second *Tikun* of *Z"A* is expressed by the lights that come out of him, as the hair on his head, and on his face. There are also

Nimin and these *Tikunim* are similar to the ones of *Arikh Anpin,* but with some differences. The hairs of *Z"A* are black and intermingled; being more of the aspect of *Gevurah*, the hairs of *Arikh Anpin* are white, and express bounty.

There are also *Nimin* of *Nukvah*; they are fifteen and their color is purple.

ניצוץ
Nitsuts
Spark
One of the 288 sparks (*Nitsutsot*).

ניצוצות
Nitsutsot
Sparks
In the emanation of the lights from the eyes of *Adam Kadmon*, first the individual *Keli* (recipient) for each *Sephira* came out and then their lights. Each one of these *Sephirot* had its own *Keli,* but the seven lower *Sephirot* were aligned one under the other in a straight line, and not ready for the guidance of kindness, rigor and mercy. Therefore, they could not contain their lights and broke.

The three first *Sephirot*: *Keter*, *'Hokhma* and *Binah*, were structured in the three-column order: B ^{K} H, their lower parts did not contain their lights, fell but did not break. These lower parts correspond to what is needed for the guidance of the seven lower *Sephirot*, if they had contained their lights, the seven *Sephirot* would not have broken, and the notions of *Kilkul* (damage) and *Tikun* (repair) not existed.

This caused an important damage called *Shvirat HaKelim* – *the breaking of the vessels*. The *Kelim* (recipients) of the seven *Sephirot* which did not contain their lights, fell to the world of

162

Beriah (creation), the lights also descended, but stayed in the world of *Atsilut*. The breaking of the *Kelim* caused a descent of all the worlds. However, *KHB* remained in what is called the "first *Atsilut*". The seven lower *Kelim* fell in the higher parts of the world of *Beriah*.

The roots of all the created are in the seven lower *Sephirot* (*Za"T*), the three first *Sephirot* are like a crown on the *Za"T* to repair and direct them. In the three first *Sephirot* there is not really a notion of damage, they are above men's deeds, and are not affected by their sins.

To sustain the *Kelim* after they broke, 288 sparks of their lights came down as well, because a connection to their original lights was needed to keep them alive.

It is important to understand that all that happens in our world, is similar to what occurred in this fall.

The goal of all the works, deeds and prayers of men in this existence, is to help and participate in the ascent of the fallen 288 sparks to their origin. This can be done by accomplishing the *Mitsvot* and the *Tefilot*. At the completion of this *Tikun* of unification between all the fallen sparks and their *Kelim*, it will be the time of the resurrection of the dead and the arrival of *Moshia'h*.
See Shvirat HaKelim, Tikun, Tefilah

נמשך
Nimshakh
Drawn
See Hamshakhah

נמשל
Nimshal
Moral
Sometimes used to explain or illustrate difficult concepts.

נסירה

Nesirah

Cutting – Separation

When *Partsuf (configuration) Zeir Anpin* is being built, *Partsuf Nukvah* is attached to his back. Once the *Partsuf Zeir Anpin* constructed, the construction of *Nukvah* starts with the lights given to her by *Partsuf Abah, Imah* and *Zeir Anpin*. She needs to separate completely from him and come to a face to face position, for a possibility of *Zivug* (union).

At first, the *Nukvah* separates from him to get her own *Mo'hin* (brains), and there is *Nesirah* (cutting off).

She is now complete, separated from *Z"A,* and can act as an independent *Partsuf.* Her rears being complete in the aspects of *Gevurot,* and the rears of *Z"A* in the aspects of *'Hasadim,* they are now face to face and ready for their various *Zivugim (*unions).

See Partsuf, Zivug, Tikun, Partsuf Z"A, Nukvah

נפילה

Nefilah

Fall

See Shvirat HaKelim, Nitsutsot

נפש

Nefesh

Soul - First level of the soul

The soul has five names: *Nefesh, Rua'h, Neshama, 'Hayah* and *Ye'hidah,* which correspond to its five levels. The soul is the spiritual entity inside the body, the latter being only his outer garment.

Since it is men that provoke the union of the four worlds, it is necessary for their souls to have their origin from them, and from the five *Partsufim:*

Soul / Level	Partsuf	World
Nefesh	Nukvah	'Asiah
Rua'h	Zeir Anpin	Yetsirah
Neshama	Imah	Beriah
'Hayah	Abah	Atsilut
Ye'hidah	Arikh Anpin	Atsilut

Each level of the soul is subdivided in five levels. As for the level of *Nefesh;* there are *Nefesh* of *Nefesh, Rua'h* of *Nefesh, Neshama* of *Nefesh, 'Hayah* of *Nefesh* and *Ye'hidah* of *Nefesh.*

Each one of these levels of the soul subdivides for each level of *Partsuf* and for each world. Therefore, there are five levels of the souls for *Partsuf Nukvah* and there are five levels of *Partsufim* for the world of *'Asiah* etc. Also, as there are in each world ten *Sephirot,* each soul has its origin corresponding to one of them.

Therefore, a soul could be from the level of *Nefesh* of *Malkhut* of *Nukvah* of *'Asiah,* or *Rua'h* of *'Hesed* of *Abah* of *'Yetsirah,* or *Neshama* of *Abah* of *Z"A* of *Yetsirah* etc.

Nefesh is the first level and is acquired before the next levels.

The higher levels of the soul cannot be acquired at once. Most men only have the level of *Nefesh,* and if they merit, they will acquire the next levels - but one by one.

To reach the next higher level of his soul, man must do the *Tikun* of the preceding level. If he needs to acquire the level of *Imah* of *'Asiah,* he must first do the *Tikun* of *Malkhut* of *'Asiah* and *Z"A* of *'Asiah,* and so on. To acquire his level of *Neshama,* he must do the *Tikun* of all the levels of the *Sephirot* and *Partsufim* of his *Nefesh* and *Rua'h* etc.

נפש, רוח, נשמה
Nefesh, Rua'h, Neshama
Three first levels of the soul.

נפש, רוח, נשמה, חיה, יחידה
Nefesh, Rua'h, Neshama, 'Hayah and Ye'hidah
The soul has five names: *Nefesh*, *Rua'h*, *Neshama*, *'Hayah* and *Ye'hidah*, which correspond to its five levels. The soul is the spiritual entity inside the body, the latter being only his outer garment.

Since it is men that provoke the union of the four worlds, it is necessary for their souls to have their origin from them, and from the five *Partsufim*:

Soul / Level	Partsuf	World
Nefesh	Nukvah	'Asiah
Rua'h	Zeir Anpin	Yetsirah
Neshama	Imah	Beriah
'Hayah	Abah	Atsilut
Ye'hidah	Arikh Anpin	Atsilut

Each level of the soul is subdivided in five levels. As for the level of *Nefesh;* there are *Nefesh* of *Nefesh*, *Rua'h* of *Nefesh*, *Neshama* of *Nefesh*, *'Hayah* of *Nefesh* and *Ye'hidah* of *Nefesh*.
Each one of these levels of the soul subdivides for each level of *Partsuf* and for each world. Therefore, there are five levels of the souls for *Partsuf Nukvah* and there are five levels of *Partsufim* for the world of *'Asiah* etc. Also, as there are in each world ten *Sephirot*, each soul has its origin corresponding to one of them. Therefore, a soul could be from the level of *Nefesh* of *Malkhut* of

166

Nukvah of *'Asiah,* or *Rua'h* of *'Hesed* of *Abah* of *'Yetsirah,* or *Neshama* of *Abah* of *Z"A* of *Yetsirah* etc.

The higher levels of the soul cannot be acquired at once. Most men only have the level of *Nefesh,* and if they merit, they will acquire the next levels - but one by one.

To reach the next higher level of his soul, man must do the *Tikun* of the preceding level. If he needs to acquire the level of *Imah* of *'Asiah,* he must first do the *Tikun* of *Malkhut* of *'Asiah* and *Z"A* of *'Asiah,* and so on. To acquire his level of *Neshama,* he must do the *Tikun* of all the levels of the *Sephirot* and *Partsufim* of his *Nefesh* and *Rua'h* etc.

See *Nefesh, Rua'h, Neshama, Hayah* and *Ye'hidah*

נפשות

Nefashot

Souls (first level)

Aspect of *Nefashot* means lowest level.

נצח

Netsa'h

Sephira (splendor)

Seventh of the *Sephirot.*

Quality: Diminished kindness to who is deserving.

Column: Right – *'Hesed* (kindness)

Position: Right – bottom

Other *Sephirot* on the same column: *'Hokhma, 'Hesed.*

Partsufim made from this *Sephira:*

One of the *Sephirot* that make the *Partsuf Z"A.*

Corresponding name: YKVK *Tsebaot*

יהו-ה -צבאות

Corresponding *Miluy* (spelling) of name: *MaH* (45) (מה)

Corresponding vowel: *'Hirik*

Physical correspondence: Right leg

Level of the soul: *Rua'h*

See Sephira, Partsuf

נצח, הוד, יסוד
Netsa'h, Hod and Yesod

Third triplet of the *Sephirot,* they mostly act together as the interior *Mo'hin* (brains) for a lower *Partsuf* (configuration) to direct him, and are called by their initials; *NHY*

The *Mo'hin (brains)* are the directive force given to the *Partsuf.* There are interior and encircling *Mo'hin.* The interior *Mo'hin* are the *Sephirot NHY (Netsa'h, Hod, Yesod)* of the superior *Partsuf,* and are composed of nine parts. They enter inside the lower *Partsuf* to be his brains or intelligence and spread in its nine *Sephirot* from *'Hokhma to Yesod.* The encircling *Mo'hin* which are the other *Sephirot; HGT ('Hesed, Gevurah, Tiferet)* and *HBD ('Hokhma, Binah, Da'at)* encircle him on the outside.

The *Mo'hin* usually come in the lower *Partsuf* in three stages. First, the *NHY* enter followed by the *HGT,* and finally the *HBD.* When the *NHY* of the higher *Partsuf* are clothed inside the lower *Partsuf,* it is given to the higher *Partsuf* new *NHY* to be complete again.

See Mo'hin, Zeir Anpin, Zivug, Gadlut

נקבה
Nekevah
Female – Feminine

Rigor is manifested by all the feminine aspects and by the concealment of the masculine aspects, which represent bounty.

Some *Partsufim* are masculine and bestow kindness, others are feminine and bestow rigor.

The *Zivug* is the union of the masculine with its feminine. All the outcomes of the higher emanations are a result of the different unions of these masculine and feminine lights.

The masculine corresponds to 'Hesed and MaH *(45)*, the feminine to Gevurah and BaN *(52)*. The Tikun (rectification) is only possible by the Zivug (union) of the masculine and the feminine.

The guidance of the world is dependent on the different positioning and interaction of the masculine and feminine Partsufim, since they have a direct effect on the measure and balance of the factors of kindness, rigor and mercy.

See Nukvah, Malkhut

נקוד

Nekud

Point

See 'Olam HaNekudim

נקודה

Nekudah

Point – Dot

When Partsuf (configuration) Zeir Anpin is being built, Partsuf Nukvah is attached to his back, and her state corresponds to one dot. When Z"A ascends, she ascends with him, during the gestation, the suckling and the growth.

During the gestation, she is attached to his Sephira Yesod, (she is still as one dot), during the suckling, she is on his Tiferet, and during the growth, she is on his Da'at. It is only once his construction complete, that Z"A starts to build Nukvah by his NHY *(Netsa'h, Hod, Yesod)* for her to be an independent Partsuf.

During the night Nukvah of the world of Atsilut (emanation) descends in the world of Beriah (creation) and corresponds to a dot. During the morning Tefilah of Sha'hrit we contribute to her reconstruction and her ascension back to Atsilut.

169

See Zivug

נקודות

Nekudot

Punctuation – Vowels – Points

Each vowel corresponds to a *Sephira*. It in a way translates, with the combination of the letters, the inner identity of the word.

Vowel	Sephira
Kamatz	Keter
Pata'h	'Hokhma
Tsere	Binah
Segol	'Hesed
Shevah	Gevurah
'Holam	Tiferet
'Hirik	Netsa'h
Kubutz	Hod
Shuruk	Yesod
No vowel	Malkhut

See Autiot

נקודים

Nekudim

Points

See 'Olam HaNekudim

נר"ן

NaRaN

Nefesh, Rua'h, Neshama

Initials of the first three levels of the souls.

נרנח"י

NRNHY

Nefesh, Rua'h, Neshama, Hayah and Ye'hidah
Initials of the five levels of the souls.

נשמה

Neshama

Soul - Third level of the soul
The soul has five names: *Nefesh*, *Rua'h*, *Neshama*, *'Hayah* and *Ye'hidah*, which correspond to its five levels. The soul is the spiritual entity inside the body, the latter being only his outer garment.

Since it is men that provoke the union of the four worlds, it is necessary for their souls to have their origin from them, and from the five *Partsufim (configurations)*:

Soul / Level	Partsuf	World
Nefesh	*Nukvah*	*'Asiah*
Rua'h	*Zeir Anpin*	*Yetsirah*
Neshama	*Imah*	*Beriah*
'Hayah	*Abah*	*Atsilut*
Ye'hidah	*Arikh Anpin*	*Atsilut*

Each level of the soul is subdivided in five levels. As for the level of *Nefesh;* there are *Nefesh* of *Nefesh*, *Rua'h* of *Nefesh*, *Neshama* of *Nefesh*, *'Hayah* of *Nefesh* and *Ye'hidah* of *Nefesh*.
Each one of these levels of the soul subdivides for each level of *Partsuf* and for each world. Therefore, there are five levels of the souls for *Partsuf Nukvah* and there are five levels of *Partsufim* for the world of *'Asiah* etc. Also, as there are in each world ten *Sephirot*, each soul has its origin corresponding to one of them.

Therefore, a soul could be from the level of *Nefesh* of *Malkhut* of *Nukvah* of *'Asiah,* or *Rua'h* of *'Hesed* of *Abah* of *'Yetsirah,* or *Neshama* of *Abah* of *Z"A* of *Yetsirah* etc.

Neshama is the third level and can be acquired only after acquiring the level of *Nefesh* and *Rua'h.*

The higher levels of the soul cannot be acquired at once. Most men only have the level of *Nefesh,* and if they merit, they will acquire the next levels - but one by one. To reach the next higher level of his soul, man must do the *Tikun* of the preceding level. If he needs to acquire the level of *Imah* of *'Asiah,* he must first do the *Tikun* of *Malkhut* of *'Asiah* and *Z"A* of *'Asiah,* and so on. To acquire his level of *Neshama,* he must do the *Tikun* of all the levels of the *Sephirot* and *Partsufim* of his *Nefesh* and *Rua'h etc*

נשמות

Neshamot

Souls

See Neshama

ס"ג

SaG (63)

Miluy (spelling) of the name י-ה-ו-ה **with a total of 63**

The creative forces or energies are the different powers in the four letters of the name of G-od י-ה-ו-ה, and the various letters added to make their different spellings. Depending on which letters are used, the numerical value of the name changes, and each one of these possibilities becomes different in its nature and actions.

The four *Miluyim* (spellings) are:

- עב ,סג , מה, בן - *'A"V, SaG, MaH, BaN*

עב – יוד הי ויו הי	*'A"V* = 72
סג – יוד הי ואו הי	*SaG* = 63
מה - יוד הא ואו הא	*MaH* = 45
בן – יוד הה וו הה	*BaN* = 52

Each name can also be divided and subdivided as:
'A"V of 'A"V, SaG of 'A"V, MaH of 'A"V …
BaN of BaN of SaG, SaG of MaH of 'A"V etc.

The name of *SaG* is the second level of the four names of *'A"V, SaG, MaH* and *BaN*. Its *Miluy* (spelling) is with the letter א י *(Yud and Aleph)* for a total of 63.

סג – יוד הי ואו הי - *SaG* = 63

ס"מ

S"M

Initials of the main destructive Angel

There are four levels of *Klipot* (husks); they are the worlds of

S'M, they obstruct the lights of the *Sephirot*, conceal man from his root and from the light.

In parallel (opposite) to the four worlds, there are four negative worlds and ten groups of negative angels divided as follows: three groups in their world of *Beriah*, six groups in *Yetsirah,* and one group in *'Asiah*. They nourish from the extremities of the higher lights, when the latter are weakened by the bad deeds of the lower beings. These destructive angels get more powers and come to do evil in the world.

See angels

סגול

Segol – Vowel E

The vowel that represents the *Sephira 'Hesed*

סגולה

Segulah

Remedy – Protection

Names, or combinations of names of angels with special signs or incantations, written on parchment

to protect, or to invoke particular powers.

By writing various permutation of letters or names of angels, one could make these superior forces act according to his will. There is a danger of using these names without a proper preparation and a good knowledge of their forces and limits.

See Kemi'a

סדר

Seder

Order

Every light or emanation has its own order of spreading.

סהר
Sahar
Moon
It is of the aspect of *Nukvah*.

סוד - סודות
Sod - ot
Secret -s
The Torah contains four levels of comprehension, of which the highest is the *Sod*. At this level, we understand that our *Tefilot* and the accomplishment of each one of the *Mitsvot*, has a direct influence on the superior worlds and on their guidance.

Through the knowledge of Kabbalah, we can get to a level of true understanding of the will of the Creator, and in a way "decode" the profound secrets of our holy Torah.

סולם
Sulam
Ladder
See *Rabbi Yehudah Ashlag*

סוף
Sof
End – Extremity
See Siyum

סיבה

Sibah

Reason – Cause

Since the intention of the Creator is to bestow goodness on His creatures, all the levels of creation were put in place so His kindness could emanate to them, yet in such a way that they would be able to receive it.

With the emanation of the lights of *MaH (45)* and *BaN (52)*, He could have done the *Tikun* (rectification) of all the worlds after the *Shvirat HaKelim (breaking of the vessels),* but then, there would not have been a reason for the participation of man in this *Tikun.* It is to give a possibility to man to act and repair the creation, that G-od restrained in a way his outflow of kindness to this world.

The reason why the Creator created these worlds, is to bestow kindness to all his creatures, and to change all evil to goodness.

סיום

Siyum

End – Extremity

From the extremity of *Sephira Malkhut* of the world of *'Asiah,* the *Sitra A'hra* (negative force) came out.

See Malkhur, Sephirot

סיטרא אחרא

Sitra A'hra

Negative force

When the *Sephirot* of BaN (52) came out from the eyes of *Adam Kadmon,* the first three *Sephirot – KHB (Keter, 'Hokhma, Binah),* took strength from the lights that came out of the ears, nose and mouth of *Adam Kadmon,* and were able to stand in three columns. The seven lower *Sephirot* did not stand in this order, they were not able to retain their lights and broke. It is only when the column of mercy stands between the columns of kindness and rigor that they can attach and bind together.

This imperfect arrangement is the first origin of the *Sitra A'hra* or "evil". This type of existence could not come to be from a perfect source; it had to originate from a defective state.

The breaking of the seven lower *Sephirot* caused a descent of all the worlds. The seven lower *Sephirot* fell in the higher parts of *Beriah*, which became the *Atsilut* of today, *Beriah* fell in the higher part of *Yetsirah*, which became the *Beriah* of today, *Yetsirah* in the higher parts of *'Asiah*, which became the *Yetsirah* of today, *'Asiah* fell even lower and became the *'Asiah* of today. From the end of *'Asiah*, the *Sitra A'hra* came out.

The *Sephirot* have their root in the *Kedushah* of the *Ein Sof*, *B'H*. The root of the *Sitra A'hra* is in the lack, or absence of the *Kedushah*. These *Klipot* (husks) obstruct the lights of the *Sephirot*, conceal man from his root and from the light.

In parallel (opposite) to the four worlds, this negative entity - *Sitra A'hra*, has its four worlds, where ten groups of negative angels divide as follows: three groups in their world of *Beriah*, six groups in *Yetsirah*, and one group in *'Asiah*. They nourish from the extremities of the higher lights when the latter are weakened by the bad deeds of the lower beings. These destructive angels get more powers and come to do evil in the world.

The existence of the *Sitra A'hra* was willed by the Creator to give man free will. With falsehood, it almost constantly tries to seduce him, and make him stumble.

The good deeds of man have an effect on the four higher worlds, his bad deeds; on the four lower worlds. It is only when man sins, that the negative side can grow in strength. In man, this negative

177

aspect grows inside him; this is his *Yetser Hara'*, it cuts him off from the higher worlds, and uproots him from the *Kedushah*.

ספירה
Sephira

The light of G-od is unique and of equal force and quality. A *Sephira* is in a way a "filter" which transforms this light in a particular force or attribute, by which the Creator guides the worlds.

Each *Sephira* is composed of a vessel called *Keli*, which holds its part of light called *Or*. There is no difference in the *Or* itself, the difference comes from the particularity, or position of the *Sephira*. There are ten *Sephirot,* their names are:

Keter
Crown

Binah		**'Hokhma**
Understanding		*Wisdom*
	Da'at	
	Knowledge	
Gevurah		**'Hesed**
Rigor		*Bounty*
	Tiferet	
	Beauty	
Hod		**Netsa'h**
Splendor		*Glory*
	Yesod	
	Foundation	
	Malkhut	
	Kingship	

On the right, the *'Hesed* (kindness*) column: 'Hokhma, 'Hesed, Netsa'h.*

In the middle, the *Ra'hamim* (mercy) *column: Keter, Tiferet, Yesod, Malkhut*

On the left, the *Din* (rigor) column: *Binah, Gevurah, Hod.*

There is one more *Sephira* called *Da'at*, which is counted when *Keter* is not, also in the *Ra'hamim* column.

The first and most important of the *Sephirot* is *Keter.* It is complete kindness to all, even to the not deserving.

The second *Sephira 'Hokhma* is also kindness to all, even to the not deserving, but less than *Keter,* and not always.

The third *Sephira Binah* is kindness to all, even to the less deserving, but from her the rigors start.

The fourth *Sephira 'Hesed* is complete kindness but to who is deserving.

The fifth *Sephira Gevurah* is full rigor to who is deserving.

The sixth *Sephira Tiferet* is kindness that makes the equilibrium between complete kindness and rigor.

The seventh *Sephira Netsa'h* is diminished kindness to who is deserving.

The eighth *Sephira Hod* is diminished rigor to who is deserving.

The ninth *Sephira* Yesod makes the equilibrium between *Sephira Netsa'h* and *Hod* for the guidance, and is the link or connection between all the superior *Sephirot* and the *Sephira Malkhut.*

The tenth *Sephira* is *Malkhut* translates all the superior emanations into one that is reflected to the creation. It is the link or connection between all the superior *Sephirot* and man.

There are also configurations of one or more *Sephirot* acting in coordination, which are called *Partsufim.*

See Partsuf, Keter, 'Hokhma, Binah, 'Hesed, Gevurah, Tiferet, Netsa'h, Hod, Yesod, Malkhut

ספירות
Sephirot
Plural of Sephira
See Sephira

ספירות הישר
Sephirot HaYashar
Straight Sephirot

After entering the *'Hallal* (vacant space) and making the ten circular *Sephirot*, the *Kav* (ray) maintained his straight shape and made ten other *Sephirot*, but this time in a linear arrangement. They were arranged in three columns: right, left and middle, representing the guidance of the world in the manner of *'Hesed, Din* and *Ra'hamim* (Kindness, rigor and mercy).

This first configuration, or the first world where the emanated lights were formed into ten *Sephirot* is called *Adam Kadmon* (*Primordial Man*). It is the union between the *Reshimu* (imprint) and the *Kav* (ray). From this first configuration, all the other worlds came forth into existence.

From this emanation, the other four worlds of *Atsilut* (emanation), *Beriah* (creation), *Yetsirah* (formation) and *'Asiah* (action) will unfold.

See Sephira, Partsuf, Hanhagah, Adam Kadmon

ספירות העיגולים
Sephirot Ha'Igulim
Encircling Sephirot

After entering the *Hallal* (vacant space), the *Kav* (ray) made ten circular *Sephirot*, encircling one another, but still maintaining a straight shape. These ten *Sephirot* are in charge of the general guidance of the worlds, and are not influenced by the actions of men.

ספירות של ב"ן
Sephirot Shel BaN
Sephirot of BaN

The lights of *BaN* (52) are of the aspect of the *'Olam HaNekudim*. From the eyes of *Adam Kadmon* came out ten *Sephirot* of the aspect of the name of *BaN* (52); ten encircling *Sephirot* from the right eye, and ten interior from the left eye, they descended lower than the navel.

They correspond to the feminine aspect - rigor, and are the root of deterioration. When they came out, the first three *Sephirot* - *KHB (Keter, 'Hokhma, Binah)*, took strength from the lights of the ears, nose and mouth of *Adam Kadmon* and were able to stand in three columns. The seven lower *Sephirot* who only took from the lights of the mouth, could not stand in this order and broke. This is called *Shvirat HaKelim* (breaking of the vessels), this imperfect arrangement is the first origin of the *Sitra A'hra* or "evil".

The *Tikun* (rectification) was done by the union of the *Sephirot* of *BaN* (52) (rigor) with the *Sephirot* of *MaH* (45) (mercy) that came out from the forehead of *Adam Kadmon*. By this union, the feminine *BaN* (52) was repaired by the masculine *MaH* (45) and made the *Partsufim* (configurations). With this new arrangement the *Sephirot* were able to stand in the three-column of kindness, rigor and mercy.

See Orot Ha'Enayim, Orot HaMetsa'h

ספירות של מ"ה
Sephirot Shel MaH
Sephirot of MaH (45)

The *Sephirot* of *MaH* (45) are of the aspect of the *'Olam HaTiKun*. After the breaking of the *Kelim* and the separation from their lights, it was necessary for the guidance of the world, that reparation be done. From the forehead of *Adam Kadmon* came out ten *Sephirot* of the aspect of the name of *MaH* (45); corresponding to the masculine - reparation. In contrast to the *Sephirot* of *BaN* (52) *which* correspond to the feminine aspect - rigor, and are the root of deterioration.

The *Tikun* was done by the union of the *Sephirot* of *MaH* (45) (mercy) and *BaN* (52) (rigor) in complex arrangements, as to allow the feminine *BaN* (52) to be repaired by the masculine *MaH* (45), and for the *Sephirot* to stand in the three-column arrangement of kindness, rigor and mercy. ith the proper order of the *Sephirot* in place, various configurations that are called *Partsufim* completed the creation.

See Orot Ha'Enayim, Orot HaMetsa'h, Partsuf

ע"ב
'A"V

'A"V Name of seventy two triplets of letters

Name hinted in the book of *Shemot* chapt 14. From the three *Pesukim* (verses) 18, 19, 20 (72 letters each) we take the first letter of *Pesuk* 18, the last of *Pesuk* 19, the first of *Pesuk* 20 and so on to get 72 triplets.

Each one of these triplets of letters as explained in the *Zohar*, has particular powers.

ע"ב
'A"V

Miluy (spelling) of the name י-ה-ו-ה with a total of 72

The creative forces or energies are the different powers in the four letters of the name of G-od י-ה-ו-ה, and the various letters added to make their different spellings. Depending on which letters are used, the numerical value of the name changes, and each one of these possibilities becomes different in its nature and actions.

The four *Miluyim* (spellings) are:

- עב ,סג , מה, בן - *'A"V , SaG, MaH, BaN*

יוד הי ויו הי – עב   - *'A"V* = 72
יוד הי ואו הי – סג   - *SaG* = 63
יוד הא ואו הא - מה   - *MaH* = 45
יוד הה וו הה – בן   - *BaN* = 52

Each name can also be divided and subdivided as:
'A"V of 'A"V, SaG of 'A"V, MaH of 'A"V …

183

BaN of BaN of SaG, SaG of MaH of 'A"V etc.

The name of *'A"V* is of the highest level of the four names of *'A"V, SaG, MaH (45)* and *BaN (52)*. Its *Miluy* (spelling) is with the letter **'** *(Yud)* for a total of 72.

עב – יוד הי ויו הי   -   *'A"V* = 72

The highest world of *Atsilut* is of the aspect of the name of *'A"V.*

עב, סג מה, בן
'A"V, SaG, MaH, BaN
Spellings of the Name י-ה-ו-ה
'A"V (72), SaG (63), MaH (45), BaN (52)
The creative forces or energies are the different powers in the four letters of the name of G-od

י-ה-ו-ה, and the various letters added to make their different spellings. Depending on which letters are used, the numerical value of the name changes, and each one of these possibilities becomes different in its nature and actions.

The four *Miluyim* (spellings) are:
- בן ,מה , סג, עב - *'A"V, SaG, MaH, BaN* -

עב – יוד הי ויו הי   -   *'A"V* = 72
סג – יוד הי ואו הי   - *SaG* = 63
מה - יוד הא ואו הא - *MaH* = 45
בן – יוד הה וו הה   - *BaN* = 52

Each name can also be divided and subdivided as:
'A"V of 'A"V, SaG of 'A"V, MaH of 'A"V ...
BaN of BaN of SaG, SaG of MaH of 'A"V etc.
All the worlds that came out of *Adam Kadmon* by way of his apertures were of the different aspects of the four names. They

have different actions and *Tikunim,* and the *Partsufim* are constructed by the union of *BaN (52)* and *MaH (45).*

See BaN, MaH, SaG, 'A"V

עבודה

'Avodah

Service – Duty

After the *Shvirat HaKelim* – the breaking of the vessels. The *Kelim* (recipients) of the seven *Sephirot* which did not contain their lights, fell to the lower worlds.

To sustain these *Kelim* after they broke, 288 sparks of their lights came down as well, because a connection to their original lights was needed to keep them alive. These sparks correspond to the four aspects of *'A"V* of the names *'A"V* (72), *SaG* (63), *MaH (45)*, *BaN (52)* , 4 x 72 = 288.

It is important to understand that all that happens in our world, is similar to what occurred in this fall.

The goal of all the works, deeds and prayers of men in this existence, is to help and participate in the ascent of the fallen 288 sparks to their origin. This can be done by accomplishing the *Mitsvot* and the *Tefilot.* At the completion of this *Tikun* of unification between all the fallen sparks and their *Kelim*, it will be the time of the resurrection of the dead and the arrival of *Moshia'h.*

See Shvirat HaKelim, Tikun, Tefilah

עבר

'Avar

Past

There is a higher dimension where there is not a notion called time. Past, present and future are one. Man being a limited entity physically and temporally, it is not possible for him to comprehend this reality.

Everything, past, present and future has a purpose, and in the end, all will be clear and comprehensible.

עובר

'Over

Passing

There is passing when lights "travel" from one position to another.

The second *Tikun* (action) of *Partsuf Arikh Anpin* is revealed by the passing of the seven lower *Sephirot* of *Partsuf 'Atik* into its head, before they are clothed in him.

The lights of a higher world have to pass through a curtain to make the *Partsufim* of a lower world.

עולם

'Olam

World

A *'Olam* is a possibility and a type of existence, in a particular dimension.

From the first configuration; *Adam Kadmon* (*Primordial man*), emanations made the four lower worlds. There is a screen (divider) that separates one world from another, and from this screen the ten *Sephirot* of the lower world came out from the ten *Sephirot* of the higher world.

The first world to unfold from *Adam Kadmon* (*Primordial man*) is called *Atsilut;* the world of emanation, where there is no existence of the separated, and no *Sitra A'hra* (*negative force*) even at its lowest levels. The second world is *Beriah* (*creation*); the world of the *Neshamot*; of the souls. The third world is *Yetsirah* (*formation*); the world of formation, the world of the angels. The fourth world is *'Asiah* (*action*); the world of action, the world of physical existence

Atsilut is of the aspect of *Partsuf Abah*, *Beriah* of *Imah*, *Yetsirah* of *Z"A,* and *'Asiah* of *Nukvah.*

See Atsilut, Beriah, Yetsirah, Asiah

עולם הברודים

'Olam Haberudim

World of reparation

After the lights of the aspect of *BaN* *(52)* and the breaking of the *Kelim* (recipients), lights of the aspect of *MaH* *(45)* came out through the forehead of *Adam Kadmon.* The union between the lights of *MaH,* which represent mercy, with the ones of *BaN,* which represent rigor, made the *Tikun* (rectification) of the broken *Sephirot.*

This *Tikun* is also the arrangement of the *Sephirot* in three columns, which will allow the beginning of the construction of the first *Partsufim.*

See Shvirat HaKelim, Tikun

עולם הנקודים

'Olam HaNikudim

The world of points

The *Sephirot* that came out through the eyes of *Adam Kadmon* were of the aspects of the *Nekudim* (punctuation), and of the name of *BaN* *(52).* This world is called the world of points because these *Sephirot* had their own *Kelim* (recipients), but were separated.

When the lights of *BaN* *(52)* came out, the *Kelim* were not in the three pillar arrangement needed for the direction of Kindness, rigor and mercy. Therefore, they could not hold the influx of these lights and broke.

See Shvirat HaKelim

187

עולם העקודים

'Olam Ha'Akudim

The world of the attached

In the *'Olam Ha'Akudim* (the attached), when the *Sephirot* came out the first time from the mouth of *Adam Kadmon*, each one had its own place, but in one unique *Keli* (recipient).

The seven lower *Sephirot* were aligned one under the other in a straight line, not in the three pillar arrangement and not ready for the guidance of kindness, rigor and mercy.

They could not hold in this configuration, and the most tenuous part of the lights returned to their origin in the mouth but not completely, each one leaving its trace. The parts of the lights that remained thickened, but were still illuminated by their own parts that ascended. The lights strike each other and produced sparks which formed the *Kelim* (recipients) for the more tenuous lights that returned a second time.

This is considered as an annulment, but not as important as the one in *'Olam HaNikudim.*

עולמות

'Olamot

Worlds

See *'Olam*

עונש

'Onesh

Punishment

From the world of *Atsilut* unfolded all the lower worlds. The last world to unfold is *'Asiah*; the physical world with the possibility of reward, punishment and evil.

There are two main kinds of guidance: The general guidance and the variable guidance.

The general guidance is for the subsistence of the worlds and is not influenced by the actions of men. This guidance is by the encircling *Sephirot.* The variable guidance is on the basis of justice, reward and punishment and is dependant on the actions of man. This guidance is by the linear *Sephirot.*

If there was only good in this world, the guidance based on the duality of reward and punishment would not be necessary, but then, men will not have free choice, and no merit for the accomplishment of the will of G-od.

עורף

'Oref

Back of the neck

Highest part on the back until where the *Klipot* (husks) can attach.

See Klipa

עיבור

'Ibur

Attachment – Gestation

There is *'Ibur* as gestation for the *Partsufim* (configurations), and *'Ibur* as attachment for the soul.

Gestation - All the *Tikunim* (rectification) of the *Partsufim* (masculine and feminine) are achieved by way of *Zivug* (union), *'Ibur* (gestation) and *Leida* (birth).

Attachment - The *Tikun* of the soul is realized by the *Gilgul* (reincarnation), and by the *'Ibur* (attachment). By accomplishing what he did not accomplish of the 613 *Mitsvot*, man makes the necessary *Tikun* of his soul which can now elevate to the higher realms and rejoin its source.

The *Gilgul* is the reincarnation of a soul from the time of birth until death, the *'Ibur* is an attachment of another soul to his, that could come and leave anytime.

For the *Mitsvot* that it was obligated to accomplish, it accomplishes them by the *Gilgul*, for the ones it did not have to accomplish, it accomplishes them by the *'Ibur,* which departs afterwards.

To help him accomplish the missing *Mitsvot*, another soul could attach to his soul (*'Ibur*), until he accomplishes it, and then departs. The missing *Mitsva* could be one he chose not to do, or one he could not do in his previous life.

עיגול

'Igul

Circle - Circular

See 'Hallal, Sephirot Ha'Igulim

עיגולים

'Igulim

Circles - Circular

See Sephirot Ha'Igulim

עיניים

'Enayim

Eyes

The lights of the aspect of *BaN (52)* came out through the eyes of *Adam Kadmon.*

See Orot Ha'Enayim, Orot Shel BaN

עיקר

'Ikar

Essential

The *Taffel* (accessory) is always subordinate to the *'Ikar*, which is the main or the essential. Likewise, some emanations are subordinate to other more important lights.

על

'Al

On – On top of

Sometimes, more important *Partsufim* (configurations) are described as being on top of other lower *Partsufim*. In reality, this only denotes a position of superiority, since more important *Partsufim* are usually clothed inside lower *Partsufim*.

See Partsuf

עליה

'Aliyah

Elevation – Ascent

There is ascent when there is reparation or amelioration.

The first ascent was the one of the *Malkin* (Kings), representing the *Kelim* (recipients) of the *Sephirot* that broke from *Beriah* to *Atsilut*.

There is also an ascent of the worlds during the *Tefilot*, when the worlds of *Asiah*, *Yetsirah* and *Beriah* ascend until *Atsilut* during the *'Amidah*.

See Tefilah, Kavanah

עליון

'Elyon

Higher – Superior

Sometimes, more important *Partsufim* are described as being on top or higher than other *Partsufim*. In reality, this only denotes a position of superiority, since more important *Partsufim* are usually clothed inside lower *Partsufim*.

See Partsuf

עליונים

'Elyonim

Higher – Superiors

See 'Elyon

עלמא

'Alma

World

See 'Olam

עמר

'Omer

Counting of the 'Omer

During the counting of the *'Omer* we rebuild during the 49 days, the seven parts of the seven *Sephirot* of *Partsuf Z"A* from *'Hesed* to *Malkhut* (7 x 7 = 49).

עמר נקי

'Amer Naki

Fifth of seven Tikunim of the head of Arikh Anpin

From the head of *Partsuf* (configuration) *Arikh Anpin,* seven emanations come out to act and influence on the guidance, called the *Tikunim* of *Arikh Anpin*.

ענן דול

'Anan Gadol - A large cloud

One of the four main levels of *Klipot* corresponding to the four lower worlds.

See Klipot

ענני כבוד

'Anane Kavod

The Clouds of Glory

Diagonal light or *Partsuf,* on the right side of *Partsuf Z"A.*
This light, or *Partsuf* is not considered as a complete *Partsuf,* its
actions are temporary and at particular times only.

ענף

'Anaf

Branch

Light or *Sephira* that is an outcome of a root.

ענפי א"ק

'Anafe A"K

Branches of Adam Kadmon

Adam Kadmon being at such close proximity to the *Ein Sof*
(infinite), we cannot grasp anything of its nature. Our
understanding only starts from the emanations that came out of
him in the way of his senses, which are called his branches.
These four branches are called: sight, hearing, smell and speech.
They spread out from his eyes, ears, nose, and mouth. In the
language of Kabbalah we use names of body parts solely to
describe the inner sense, or the position they represent. It is
understood, of course, that there is no physical existence at
these level. These four emanations are of the aspects of the
names of *'A"V (72), SaG (63), MaH (45)* and *BaN (52).*
From the eyes, came out lights of the aspect of the name *BaN
(52).* These feminine lights caused the *Shvirat HaKelim*
(breaking of the vessels).
From the forehead, came out lights of the aspect of the name of
MaH (45), these masculine lights will make the *Tikun*
(rectification) of the broken *Sephirot,* and together with *BaN*
make all the *Partsufim* (configurations) for the guidance of the
worlds.
From all these emanations, the other four worlds of *Atsilut*

193

(emanation), *Beriah* (creation), *Yetsirah* (formation) and *'Asiah* (action) will unfold.

ענפים
'Anafim
Branches
Lights or *Sephirot* that are an outcome of a root.

עסמ"ב
'ASMaB
'A"V *(72)*, **SaG** *(63)*, **MaH** *(45)*, **BaN** *(52)*
Initials

עפר
'Afar
Soil – Dust
The body is called soil. It obstructs the spiritual aspect, which is the *Neshama,* from seeing and understanding.

עץ הדעת טוב ורע
'Ets Hada'at Tov ve Ra'
The Tree of Knowledge of Good and Bad
The *Bne* Israel went in exile in Egypt to make the *Tikun* (rectification) of "'*Ets Hada'at*" which is of the aspect of *Yesod* of *Partsuf Z"A* .

עץ החיים
'Ets Ha'Haim
Tree of Life
It is of the aspect of *Tiferet* of *Partsuf Z"A.*
During the night the "Tree of Life" ascends higher and the "Tree of death" governs,. It is only in the morning that the governance is given back to the Tree of Life and that all the souls return in

194

men's bodies. (Zohar, Bamidbar)

It is also the name of the master work of the Ari Z'al.

See Ari Z'al

עצם השמים

'Etsem HaShamayim

Name of a *Hekhal (portal).*

Second of seven *Hekhalot,* corresponding to *Hod.*

The *Hekhalot* are the different levels of ascension of the *Tefilot* (prayers) before reaching the final seventh *Hekhal* (portal); *Kodesh Hakodashim.*

עצמות

'Atsmut

Essence – Nature

The inner light of each *Sephira* or *Partsuf* is identical. The lights are transformed only once inside, by the nature of the *Sephira* or *Partsuf.*

עקב

'Ekev

Heel

Some *Neshamot* came out from the heel of *Adam Kadmon,* corresponding to a left part of *Kayin.*

עקודים

'Akudim

Bound - Tied

See Olam Ha'Akudim

ערב רב

'Erev Rav

The mixed multitude

Diagonal light or *Partsuf* on the right side of *Ya'acov.*
This light, or *Partsuf*, is not considered as a complete *Partsuf*; its
actions are temporary and at particular times only.

ערבים
'Arevim
Guarantors - Mutual responsibility
"*Kol Israel 'Arevim ze la ze*", every Jew is a guarantor for his
fellow Jew. The majority of the *Tikunim* (rectifications), as
explained in the Kabbalah, are not realized by one, but more by
the actions of many. The *Geulah* (liberation) will come as a
result of the efforts of all Israel.

ערלה
'Orla
Foreskin
When the *'Orla* covers the *Sephira Yesod*, the *'Hasadim* cannot
spread from the chest and down. Similarly, the foreskin has to be
removed from the masculine organ which is also called the
Yesod.

עשו
'Essav
Diagonal light or *Partsuf* on the left side of *Ya'acov.*
This light, or *Partsuf*, is not considered as a complete *Partsuf*; its
actions are temporary and at particular times only.

עשיה
'Asiah
World of action – of man
From the first configuration of *Adam Kadmon,* four worlds
unfolded.
On these four worlds, the four letters of the Name (י-ה-ו-ה) *B'H,*

govern.

' in *Atsilut;* by it, all the repaired levels are put in order.

ה descends from it (*Atsilut*) to *Beriah,* and guides it.

ו to *Yetsirah,* and

ה to *'Asiah.*

The fourth world to unfold is called *'Asiah* - action, the world of physical existence.

It is under *Atsilut, Beriah* and *Yetsirah.*

It consists of five main *Partsufim: Arikh Anpin, Abah, Imah, Zeir Anpin* and *Nukvah.* One more *Partsuf, 'Atik Yomin,* is on top of them.

There is a screen (divider) that separates one world from another. From this screen, the ten *Sephirot* of the lower world come out from the ten *Sephirot* of the higher world. The three superior worlds of *Atsilut, Beriah* and *Yetsirah,* are interior to the fourth world of *'Asiah.*

In parallel to the four worlds (*ABYA*), there are four types of existence in our world; mineral corresponding to *'Asiah (action),* vegetal corresponding to *Yetsirah (formation),* animal corresponding to *Beriah (creation),* and man corresponding to *Atsilut (emanation).*

The world of *'Asiah* is of the aspect of *BaN (52).* Thus, *'Asiah* is of the aspect of *Partsuf Nukvah – Sephira Malkhut.*

עשר

'Eser

Ten

Number of *Sephirot* in each world, in each *Sephira, Partsuf* or configuration.

עשר מכות
'Eser Makot
Ten plagues
Each plague corresponds to a *Sephira*.

עת
'Et
Time – Moment
Each moment can be described in term of permutation of the names of G-od, and by the various *Sephirot and Partsufim*.

עת רצון
'Et Ratson
Moment of bounty
Time when the configuration of bounty is prevailing. One of them is at the time of *Min'ha* of *Shabbat*.
See Tefilah

עתיד
'Atid
Future
There is a higher dimension where there is not a notion called time. Past, present and future are one. Man being a limited entity physically and temporally, it is not possible for him to comprehend this reality.
Everything, past, present and future has a purpose, and in the end, all will be clear and comprehensible.
See Giluy Yi'hudo

עתיק
'Atik
Partsuf – Ancient
Sometimes *Partsuf 'Atik Yomin* is only called *'Atik*.

See 'Atik Yomin

עתיק יומין

'Atik Yomin

Partsuf – Ancient

The *Partsuf 'Atik* is superior to all the *Partsufim*. It was constructed by the *Zivug* (union) of *'A"V* and *SaG* of *Adam Kadmon*. It has ten *Sephirot*, its aspect of *MaH* (45) corresponds to the masculine principle, its aspect of *BaN* (52) to the feminine, it is called *'Atik* and his *Nukvah*. Its *Nukvah* is never separated from him, her back attached to his back, *'Atik* is thus all face; the face of *BaN* (52) corresponding to its back, the face of *MaH* (45) to its front.

Its masculine aspect is not clothed inside *Atsilut*. The first three *Sephirot* of his *Nukvah* are above *Atsilut,* and make together the *Radl'a* - רישה דלא אתידע (the unknown head). Its seven lower *Sephirot* dress inside *Partsuf Arikh Anpin*.

The *Partsuf 'Atik* makes the connection between the worlds, in *Atsilut* it is the *Malkhut* of *Adam Kadmon* which becomes its *Partsuf 'Atik*. It is the same in the three other worlds of *Beriah*, *Yetsirah* and *'Asiah,* the *Malkhut* of the world above becomes the *Partsuf 'Atik* of the world below.

See Partsuf

עתיקא

'Atika

Partsuf Arikh Anpin

In the two *Adarot* of Rabbi Shim'on Bar Yo'hay in the *Zohar*, *Arikh Anpin* is called *'Atika*.

See Partsuf Arikh Anpin

פאה
Peah
Edge or side of the face
See Shete Peot

פה פנוי
Peh Panuy
Free mouth
Peh Panuy is the twelfth of the thirtheen *Tikunim* (action) of the *Dikna* (beard) of *Partsuf Arikh Anpin,* it corresponds to the free mouth. The *Dikna* reveals the guidance of kindness, rigor and mercy.

פנים
Panim
Face or Front
Closeness or readiness.

פנים באחור
Panim B A'hor
Face to back
There is a notion of closeness and interaction, depending on whether the *Partsufim* (configurations) face or turn their back to each other. The three possibilities are: face to face, face to back, or back to back.
Face to back denotes a readiness to get close from one side only. It is a position of waiting or longing for the face to face, which is the ideal situation. The guidance of the world is dependent on the different positioning and interaction of these masculine and feminine *Partsufim*, since they have a direct effect on the measure and balance of the factors of kindness, rigor and mercy.

פנים בפנים

Panin B Panim

Face to Face

There is a notion of closeness and interaction, depending on whether the *Partsufim* (configurations) face or turn their back to each other. The three possibilities are: face to face, face to back, or back to back.

Face to face is the ideal level and corresponds to the bestowing of abundance.

When the *Partsuf Nukvah* is ready for the *Zivug* (union), she comes face to face with the masculine; this is the ideal positioning for the *Zivug*.

The guidance of the world is dependent on the different positioning and interaction, of these masculine and feminine *Partsufim*, since they have a direct effect on the measure and balance of the factors of kindness, rigor and mercy.

פנימי

Pnimi

Inner – Internal

There are interior aspects, and exterior aspects. All the lights subdivide among themselves in interiority and exteriority aspects. Depending on the context, the exterior or the interior aspect could be superior.

פנימיות

Pnimiut

Internality

What is inside or interior. Also applies to deeper meaning or spirituality.

See *Pnimi*, *Or Pnimi*, *Keli Pnimi*, *Partsuf*

פסול

Pasul

Disqualified

State of distance from the *Kedushah* and closeness to the *Sitra A'hra* (negative force).

פעולה

Pe'ulah

Action

The Kabbalah teaches us that the world is guided by an extremely complex system of forces or lights. By their actions or interactions, are provoked chain reactions that impact directly on man and the worlds.

Each one of these actions has numerous ramifications, with many details and results.

פקיחו דעינין

Peki'hu De'inin

Sixth of the seven Tikunim of the head of Arikh Anpin

From the head of *Partsuf* (configuration) *Arikh Anpin,* seven emanations come out to act and influence on the guidance, called the *Tikunim* of *Arikh Anpin.*

פרגוד

Pargod

Curtain

A curtain denotes a limit, a difference of level, or a separation of lights.

After the spreading of the lights and the unfolding of the worlds, lights collided at the bottom of the world of *Atsilut*. A curtain was made between *Atsilut* and *Beriah* by the striking of these lights. From there, other *Partsufim* similar to the ones in *Atsilut* were formed in the lower worlds, but of a lower force since the lights were dimmed by the divider.

פרסא

Parsa

Curtain

See Pargod

פרצוף

Partsuf

Configuration - Countenance

The light of G-od is unique and of equal force and quality. A *Sephira* is in a way a "filter" which transforms this light in a particular force or attribute, by which the Creator guides the worlds. A *Partsuf* is a configuration of one or more *Sephirot* acting in coordination.

Some *Partsufim* are masculine and bestow kindness, others are feminine and bestow rigor. The masculine corresponds to '*Hesed* and *MaH* (45), the feminine to *Gevurah* and *BaN* (52). By their union, different equilibriums of these two forces (Kindness and rigor), make the guidance. Complete rigor will be the destruction of anything not perfect, while complete kindness will permit everything without restriction. However, these two aspects are necessary for the guidance of justice, and to give man the possibility of free choice

For the guidance, the *Tikunim* of the *Partsufim* are the actions, illuminations and inter-relations of the *Partsufim* and their influence on the worlds. These *Tikunim* result in various illuminations of different intensities, depending on time and the actions of man.

For the abundance to come down to the world, *Partsuf Zeir Anpin* needs to unite with *Nukvah*. There can be abundance only when

the masculine and the feminine are in harmony. The guidance of
the world is dependent on the different positioning and interaction
of the masculine and feminine *Partsufim*, since they have a direct
effect on the measure and balance of the factors of kindness,
rigor and mercy.

The *Partsufim* of *Zeir Anpin* and *Nukvah* are the root of all the
created. It is by their *Tikunim* that the guidance of justice is
manifested. Each day, according to the actions of man, the
Tefilot (prayers) during the week, *Shabbat* or *Holidays*, and
depending on time, various configurations allow different *Zivugim*
(unions) of *Partsufim*, and therefore outflows of abundance of
variable intensities.

There are five main *Partsufim:*
- *Arikh Anpin*
- *Abah*
- *Imah*
- *Zeir Anpin*
- *Nukvah*

And one on top of them: *'Atik Yomin* (clothed inside *Arikh Anpin*).

From these five *Partsufim;* emerge seven more. They all
emanate from the ten *Sephirot* as follows:

From *Keter:*
- *'Atik Yomin* and his ***Nukvah***
- ***Arikh Anpin*** and his ***Nukvah***

From *'Hokhma:*
- ***Abah***
- From *Malkhut* of *Abah* - ***Israel Saba***
- From *Malkhut* of *Israel Saba* - ***Israel Saba 2***

From *Binah:*
- *Imah*
- From *Malkhut* of *Binah* -***Tevunah***
- From *Malkhut* of *Tevunah* - ***Tevunah* 2**

Israel Saba and *Tevunah* are also called by their initials *ISOT* or *ISOT* 2.

From *'Hesed, Gevurah, Tiferet, Netsa'h, Hod, and Yesod:*
- ***Zeir Anpin*** also called ***Israel***
From *Zeir Anpin* - **Ya'acov**

From *Malkhut:*
- **Nukvah**, divided in two *Partsufim*: **Ra'hel and Leah**

פרצופים
Partsufim
Configurations
See *Partsuf*

פרקין
Prakin
Parts
Some *Sephirot* have three parts, while others have two. These different parts have their own interactions and illuminations.
See *Mo'hin*

פשוט
Pashut
Simple
Before the creation, G-od's light or energy is called "simple light".

Simple; because absolutely perfect, with no distinctions, measures or qualities.

At first, the Creator was alone, occupying all space with His light. His light without end or variations, filled everything. If we think about differentiations, we introduce a notion of limit, or absence of its opposite. Being ourselves distinct separate beings, we cannot grasp the concept of the "non-distinct", everything we know is finite by having a measure or an opposite. However, since the concept of limitlessness is beyond our human comprehension, we therefore have to use terms accessible to our understanding.

In Kabbalah the term 'quality' is used, to differentiate the various transformations of this "simple light", and to help us understand its effects upon the guidance of the worlds.

See Partsuf, Zivug

פתח
Pata'h

Pata'h – Vowel A
The vowel that represents the *Sephira 'Hokhma.*

פתח
Peta'h

Opening – Entrance
Entrance to a dimension. Possibility of permissibility, or understanding.

צבאות

Tsevaot

Troops - Army

Army of angels. One of the Names of G-od in combination with other names.

צדיק

Tsadik

Righteous

State of outmost closeness to the *Kedushah* and distance from the *Sitra A'hra (negative force)*. Also attributed to the *Sephira Yesod*.

צדיקים

Tsadikim

Righteous

The *Neshamot* of the ten *Tsadikim* that were killed by the Romans, have the power during the *Tefilot* (prayers) to elevate *Mayin Nukvin* (feminine waters) of the aspect of *BaN (52)*, which then provokes the descent of the *Mayin Dukhrin* (masculine waters) of the aspect of *MaH (45))*. This is essential for the preparation of the *Zivug* (union) of the *Partsufim* (configurations) during the *Tefilah*.

צו"ר ט"ק

Tsu'r T'K

There is a special force called *"Tsu'r T'K"*, that has the power to create separate entities from nothing.

This force is not related to the *Sephirot*. It was first explained is the *"Sepher HaYetsrira"*, (Book of Formation) which is one of the first Kabbalistic writing. It is only after being created that the guidance is taken over by the *Sephirot*.

צומח
Tsomea'h
Vegetal
In parallel to the four worlds of *Atsilut, Beriah, Yetsirah* and *'Asiah,* there are four types of existence in our world: mineral (דומם), vegetal (צומח), animal (חי), and the speaking (מדבר)..
Mineral corresponding to *'Asiah*, vegetal corresponding to *Yetsirah*, animal corresponding to *Beriah,* and the speaking corresponding to *Atsilut.*

צורה
Tsurah
Form
Shape or identification.

ציון
Zion
The land of Israel, the closest place to G-od's emanations.

צינור
Tsinor
Conduit
A *Sephira* is in a way a "conduit" which transforms the light in a particular force or quality, by which the Creator guides the worlds.

ציצית
Tsitsit
Fringe
The *Tsitsit* correspond to *Partsuf* (configuration) *Ra'hel.*
When *Partsuf Z"A* is in the growth stage, the *NHY* (Netsa'h, Hod, Yesod) of *Imah* come down on his back, this makes his hair (lights) come out from his head, and go downward until his chest. When

they are at the level of his thorax; it corresponds to the *Talit*, when they are at the level of *Ra'hel*; it corresponds to the *Tsitsit*.

ציר

Tsir

Axis

Two Vav and one Yud that make the *Keli* (recipient) of a *Partsuf* (configuration).

The construction of a *Partsuf* is done by the twenty two letters. For the construction of *Nukvah*, twenty two letters and five ending letters: מנצפך, (five *Gevurot* - rigors), are given to her by *Partsuf* *Z"A* and *Imah*. Once they build her, they end in her *Yesod* and make a *Keli* in the shape of the final letter *Mem* (ם).

צירי

Tsere – Vowel E

The vowel that represents the *Sephira Binah*

צל"ם

Tselem

Mo'hin (brains) of Z"A

The *Tselem* are the *Mo'hin* (brains) given to *Z"A* by the *Zivug* (union) of *Partsuf Abah* and *Imah*.

There are two distinct *Mo'hin* that come to *Z"A*, *Mo'hin* of *Imah* that arrive first, and then the *Mo'hin* of *Abah*.

Depending on the state of growth of *Z"A*, they are from *Partsuf* *ISOT*, or directly from *Abah* and *Imah*. A first part; *NHY* (Netsa'h, Hod, Yesod) of the *Mo'hin* enter inside the *Partsuf*, while the other two parts *HGT* ('Hesed, Gevurah, Tiferet) and *KHBD* (Keter, 'Hokhma, Binah, Da'at) encircle him on the outside.

There are two growths for *Partsuf Z"A*. It is only after the second growth, that *Z"A* has reached its full potential. This is *Gadlut* 2.

See *Partsuf Z"A, Mo'hin, Gadlut*

צלע

Tsela'

Rib

Representation of the *Partsuf Nukvah* in *Bereshit*. The rib taken from *Adam HaRishon*, is a description of the *Nesirah* (separation), when the *Nukvah* separates from *Z"A* to become an independent *Partsuf*.

See Nesirah

צמצום

Tsimtsum

Contraction - Retraction

In the beginning, there was no existence except His presence, the Creator was alone, occupying all space with His light. His light without end, borders or limit filled everything. He was not bestowing his influence, because there was no one to receive it. When He willed to create, He started to influence. His light being of such holiness and intensity, it is not possible for any being to exist in its proximity.

The "*Tsimtsum*" is the first act of the *Ein Sof* (Infinite) in the creation. It is the retraction of His light from a certain space and encircling it, so as to reduce its intensity and allow created beings to exist. After this contraction, a ray of His light entered this empty space and formed the first *Sephirot*.

By these boundaries, He revealed the concepts of rigor and limit, needed by the created beings, and gave a space for all the created to exist. This round space is called "'*Hallal*", and contains all possibilities of existence for separated entities, given that they are distanced from the intensity of His light.

See Kav, Rechimu, Adam Kakmon, Sephira

קבלה
Kabbalah

The Kabbalah is the mystical and esoteric explanation of the Torah. It teaches the unfolding of the worlds, the various ways of guidance of these worlds, the role of man in the creation, the will of the Creator and so on. No other writings explain in details, the creation of this world and the ones above it, the lights or energies that influence its guidance, nor the final goal of everything. These writings are based on ancient Jewish texts and mostly on the *Zohar*.

The word Kabbalah comes from the verb Lekabel (to receive), but to receive it is first necessary to want, and to become a *Keli* (recipient) able to receive and contain this knowledge.

The Kabbalah, explains to us the true guidance of the world, so that we may understand the will of G-od. How, and why He created the world, in what way He governs it, the provenance of the souls and angels, the purpose of the existence of evil, the reasons for the dualism of reward and punishment, etc.

The Kabbalah teaches us that the world is guided by an extremely complex system of forces or lights, which through their interactions, provoke chain reactions that impact directly on man and the worlds. Each one of these reactions has numerous ramifications, with many details and results.

A true understanding of the will of the Creator is possible through the knowledge of Kabbalah, which teaches us the profound secrets of our holy *Torah*, and what we are allowed to know of G-od: His will, how He guides the world, and how we can participate and influence this guidance.

The Kabbalah also demonstrates to us the importance of man, because only he, by getting closer to the Creator, can influence these incredible forces.

קבלה מעשית
Kabbalah Ma'asit
Practical Kabbalah
The "other" type of Kabbalah, where names or combinations of names of angels are used with special signs or incantations, sometimes written on parchment, to invoke particular powers and alterate normal states of events.
See Kmi'a

קדוש
Kadosh
Holly – Saintly
State of closeness to the *Kedushah* and distance from the *Sitra A'hra* (negative force).
See Kedushah

קדוש ברוך הוא
Kadosh Barukh Hu
Saintly and Blessed He is
One of the names of G-od.
The light of the *Ein Sof* (infinite) which is revealed by the *Partsuf* (configuration) *Zeir Anpin*.

קדושה
Kedushah
Sanctity – Holiness
The *Sephirot* have their root in the *Kedushah* of the *Ein Sof*, B'H.
The root of the *Sitra A'hra* (negative force) is in the lack, or absence of the *Kedushah*. Its existence was willed by the Creator to give man free will. It creates *Klipot* (husks) that attach to the exteriority of the *Sephirot*, nourish from their lights, and gain more power to act negatively
By accomplishing the *Mitsvot* and the *Tefilot* (prayers), men do

the *Tikunim* (rectifications) necessary to detach these *Klipot* from the *Kedushah*.

The ultimate goal is to create a maximum distance from the *Sitra A'hra* (negative force), and closeness to the *Kedushah*.

קדיש
Kadish

The *Kadish* makes possible the ascent of each world to the next higher world, and the descent afterwards from the world of *Atsilut* to *'Asiah*.

See Kavanah, Tefilah

קדש קדשים
Kodesh Kodashim

Name of a *Hekhal* (portal).

Seventh of seven *Hekhalot*, corresponding to *Keter, 'Hokhma* and *Binah*.

The *Hekhalot* are the different levels of ascension of the *Tefilot* (prayers) before reaching the final seventh *Hekhal* (portal); *Kodesh Hakodashim*.

קו
Kav

Ray – Line

After the *Tsimtsum*, a straight ray of light called *"Kav"*, emerged from the *Ein Sof* (infinite) and entered on one side of the *"'Hallal"* (vacant space), where there were still a *Reshimu* (imprint) of the original light. The combination of the *Kav* and the *Reshimu* is what will give existence to the *Sephirot* with which He governs the worlds.

קובוץ
Kubutz - Vowel U
The vowel that represents the *Sephira Hod.*

קודשא בריך הוא
Kudsha Berikh Hu
Saintly and Blessed He is
See Kadosh Barukh Hu

קוץ של יוד
Kots shel Yud
Extremity of the letter Yud
Superior extremity of the letter Yud of the *Tetragamon*, which represents the *Sephira Keter* or the *Partsuf Arikh Anpin.*

קורדובירו
Kordovero
Rabbi Moshe Kordovero
Born in 1522, died in Tsfat in 1570.
He was the founder of the Kabbalah academy in Tsfat, one of his best known student was Rabbi 'Haim Vital. He foresaw the coming of the teachings of the Ari Z'al and admitted in advance their truthfulness. Some of his main works are "Tomer Deborah", "Pardes Rimonim", "Or Yakar".

קטורת
Ketoret
Incense
During the *Tefilah*, by naming the eleven types of incenses used in the Temple, the *Klipot* (husks) are put aside to allow the process of ascension of the worlds.

קטן
Katan

One of the seven main types of *Gematriot.*

Tens and hundreds are reduced to one digit.

From	To	Value
א	ט	1 - 9
י	צ	1 - 9
ק	ת	1 - 4
ך	ץ	5 -9

Ex :   הארץ = 17

קטנות
Katnut
Smallness – Infancy

At first *Partsuf Z"A* is in a state of *Dormita* (somnolence), to act, it needs to get its *Mo'hin* (brains). Inside of *Imah, Partsuf Z"A* goes through a period of gestation, followed by a first and a second period of infancy.

קיפול רגלים של אריך אנפין
Kipul Reglaim shel Arikh Anpin
Folding of the legs of Arikh Anpin

After the *Shvirat HaKelim* (breaking of the vessels), when the lights were separated from their recipients, the first act of reparation for this damage was to reunite again these fallen lights and recipients.

Partsuf Arikh brought up his three lower *Sephirot – Netsa'h, Hod, Yesod* on to clothe his three higher *Sephirot - 'Hesed, Gevurah, Tiferet,* three *(NHY)* on three *(HGT).*

This was the first force given to the broken recipients of the seven *Sephirot* to ascend to their lights.

215

קליפה
Klipah
Husk (negative force)
See Klipot

קליפה נוגה
Klipah Nogah
Husk – Glow
One of the four main levels of *Klipot.*
See Klipot

קליפות
Klipot
Husks (negative forces)
The *Klipot* are the manifestation of the negative force. They obstruct the lights of the *Sephirot,* and conceal man from his root and from the light. Because of the bad deeds of the lower beings, the *Klipot* get their strength and do evil in the world by attaching to the higher lights.

The *Tikunim* (rectification) of the lower beings are to detach these *Klipot* from the *Kedushah* by accomplishing the *Mitsvot* and the *Tefilot.* When men act negatively, they cause a deterioration that reach the lower worlds and give strength to the *Klipot* to attach and nourish from the *Sephirot* of the higher worlds.

There are four main levels of *Klipot:*

- נגה - *(Nogah)* - Glow
- ענן דול - *('Anan Gadol)* - A large cloud
- אש מתלקחת - *(Eish Mitlaka'hat)* - A dividing fire
- רוח סערה - *(Rua'h She'ara)* - A wind of storm.

They correspond to the four lower worlds, which also comprise of *Sephirot* and *Partsufim* as in the positive worlds.
See Sitra A'hra

216

קלקול

Kilkul

Deterioration – Damage

Kilkul is the opposite of *Tikun* (rectification).

In the *Shvirat HaKelim* (breaking of the vessels), the *Kilkul* was caused by the disposition of the seven lower *Sephirot* in a straight line (one under the other), instead of the three-column arrangement, and when the inferior part of the three first *Sephirot* did not contain their lights.

If these *Sephirot* had contained their lights, the seven lower *Sephirot* would not have broken and all the future notions of *Kilkul* and *Tikun* not existed.

See Shvirat HaKelim

קמ"ג

KaMa"G

KM"G (143)

Miluy (spelling) of the name ה-י-ה-א, with the letter א.

אלף הא יוד הא

קמיע

Kmi'a

Amulet

Names, or combinations of names of angels, with special signs or incantations, written on parchment to protect or to invoke particular powers.

קמץ

Kamatz

Kamatz – Vowel A

The vowel that represents the *Sephira Keter*.

קנ"א

KaN"A

KN"A (151)

Miluy (spelling) of the name ה-י-ה-א, with the letter ה

אלף הה יוד הה

קס"א

KaS"A

KS"A (161)

Miluy (spelling) of the name ה-י-ה-א, with the letter י

אלף הי יוד הי

קרומא דאוירא

Kroma Deavirah

Third of seven Tikunim of the head of Arikh Anpin

From the head of *Partsuf* (configuration) *Arikh Anpin,* seven emanations come out to act and influence on the guidance, called the *Tikunim* of *Arikh Anpin.*

קשין

Kashin

Hard

Some rigors are called "דינין קשין" *(Dinin Kashim)* – Hard rigors.

קשר

Kesher

Attachment - Relation – Similitude

All the *Sephirot* and *Partsufim* have a certain degree of attachment between them.

ראיה

Reiya

Seeing

From the lights that were invested inside of *Adam Kadmon* emerged numerous worlds in the way of his senses, which are called his branches.

These "branches" are the lights that spread forth from *Adam Kadmon* by way of its apertures in the head, four of which are called: sight, hearing, smell and speech. They spread out from his eyes, ears, nose, and mouth.

The lights that came out from the eyes are of the feminine aspect of *BaN* (52), which caused the breaking of the vessels *(Shvirat HaKelim)*.

ראש

Rosh

Head

The three first *Sephirot; Keter,'Hokhma,* and *Binah* are called the head of a Partsuf.

ראשית

Reshit

Beginning – First

"The beginning of wisdom is to awe (venerate) G-od." *(Tehilim* 111, 10)

רגיל

Ragil (regular)

One of the seven main types of *Gematriot*. This one is considered as simple or regular *Gematria*, and is the most frequently used.

The numbers of the letters are as follows:

From	To	Value
א	ט	1 - 9
י	צ	10 -90
ק	ת	100 - 400
ך	ץ	500 -900

Ex :   הארץ = 1106

See Gematria

רדל"א
Radl'a
The Unknown Head
Initials of *"Reisha de lo Idtyada'"*. It is mostly called by its initials. *Partsuf 'Atik Yomin* is superior to all the *Partsufim* (configurations). In *Arikh Anpin*, are clothed the seven lower *Sephirot* of *'Atik Yomin*. The first three *Sephirot* of *Nukvah* of *'Atik Yomin: Keter, 'Hokhma* and *Binah* did not dress inside *Arikh,* and remained on top of his head, they make the *Radl'a* – the unknown head; it is called this way because we can not grasp any understanding of it.

רוח
Rua'h
Soul - Second level of the soul
The soul has five names: *Nefesh, Rua'h, Neshama, 'Hayah* and *Ye'hidah,* which correspond to its five levels. The soul is the spiritual entity inside the body, the latter being only his outer garment.
Since it is men that provoke the union of the four worlds, it is necessary for their souls to have their origin from them, and from

the five *Partsufim* (configurations):

Soul / Level	Partsuf	World
Nefesh	*Nukvah*	*'Asiah*
Rua'h	*Zeir Anpin*	*Yetsirah*
Neshama	*Imah*	*Beriah*
'Hayah	*Abah*	*Atsilut*
Ye'hidah	*Arikh Anpin*	*Atsilut*

Each level of the soul is subdivided in five levels. As for the level of *Nefesh;* there are *Nefesh* of *Nefesh, Rua'h* of *Nefesh, Neshama* of *Nefesh, 'Hayah* of *Nefesh* and *Ye'hidah* of *Nefesh.*
Each one of these levels of the soul subdivides for each level of *Partsuf* and for each world. Therefore, there are five levels of the souls for *Partsuf Nukvah* and there are five levels of *Partsufim* for the world of *'Asiah* etc. Also, as there are in each world ten *Sephirot*, each soul has its origin corresponding to one of them.
Therefore, a soul could be from the level of *Nefesh* of *Malkhut* of *Nukvah* of *'Asiah,* or *Rua'h* of *'Hesed* of *Abah* of *'Yetsirah,* or *Neshama* of *Abah* of *Z"A* of *Yetsirah* etc.
Rua'h is the second level and is acquired before the next levels.
The higher levels of the soul cannot be acquired at once. Most men only have the level of *Nefesh,* and if they merit, they will acquire the next levels - but one by one.
To reach the next higher level of his soul, man must do the *Tikun* of the preceding level. If he needs to acquire the level of *Imah* of *'Asiah*, he must first do the *Tikun* of *Malkhut* of *'Asiah* and *Z"A* of *'Asiah*, and so on. To acquire his level of *Neshama*, he must do the *Tikun* of all the levels of the *Sephirot* and *Partsufim* of his *Nefesh* and *Rua'h* etc.

רוח סערה
Rua'h Se'arah - A wind of storm
One of the four main levels of *Klipot* corresponding to the four lower worlds.

See Klipot

רוחני
Ru'hani
Spiritual
The Torah contains four levels of comprehension, of which the highest is the *Sod* (secret). At this level, we understand that our *Tefilot* and the accomplishment of each one of the *Mitsvot,* has a direct influence on the superior worlds and on their guidance.

A spiritual person will give importance to this higher meaning of things, and live in the path of rightness to strengthen himself constantly.

רוחניות
Ru'haniut
Spirituality
See Ru'hani

רושם
Roshem
Imprint –seal
See Reshimu

רזא
Secret
Raza
See Sod

רחבה של זקן
Re'hava shel Zakan
Width of the beard
Re'hava shel Zakan is the sixth of the thirtheen *Tikunim* (action) of the *Dikna* (beard) of *Arikh Anpin,* it corresponds to: The width of the beard. Each one of these *Tikunim* has its particular function or action for the general guidance.

רחוק
Ra'hok
Distant – Far
Denotes a back to back position, or an important difference in power or level.

רחל
Ra'hel
Ra'hel - Partsuf Nukvah
The *Partsuf Nukvah,* which represents the feminine – the principle of receiving, comprises of two distinct *Partsufim* (configurations): *Ra'hel* and *Leah. Partsuf Ra'hel* is of the aspect of kindness, *Partsuf Leah* of the aspect of rigor.
Partsuf Ra'hel is under *Partsuf Leah* at the level of *NHY* of *Partsuf Z"A.*
All the abundance that comes down to the world, proceeds from the various *Zivugim* (unions) of *Z"uN (Z"A* and *Nukvah).* There are five different *Zivugim:* Two with *Ra'hel* and three with *Leah.* The *Zivugim* with Ra'hel are of a higher level; being of the aspect of kindness, the ones with Leah are more of the aspect of rigor.
In the *Tefilah* of *Sha'hrit,* there is the *Zivug* of *Ya'acov* and *Ra'hel.*
In the *Tefilah* of *Musaf Shabbat,* there is the *Zivug* of *Z"A* and *Ra'hel.*
See Malkhut, Nukvah, Zivug, Kavanah

223

רחמים
Ra'hamim
Mercy
From the *Kav* (ray) ten Sephirot were formed in a linear arrangement, and later in three columns: right, left and middle, representing the guidance of the world in the manner of *'Hesed, Din* and *Ra'hamim* (Kindness, rigor and mercy). This guidance is dependent on time, and the actions of men.
The *Ra'hamim* (mercy) column is in the middle and is composed of the *Sephirot Keter, Tiferet, Yesod, Malkhut.*
Complete rigor will be the destruction of anything not perfect, while complete kindness will permit everything without restriction. *Ra'hamim* makes the balance and equilibrium between the kindness and rigor columns for a possible existence.

ריח
Reya'h
Smelling
From the lights that were invested inside of *Adam Kadmon* emerged numerous worlds in the way of his senses; which are called his branches.
These "branches" are the lights that spread forth from *Adam Kadmon*, by way of its apertures in the head, four of which are called: Sight, hearing, smell and speech. They spread out from his eyes, ears, nose, and mouth.
From the nose, came out lights of the aspect of the name of *SaG.*
See Orot Ha'Hotem

רישא דלא אתידע
Reisha de lo Ityada'
The Unknown Head
See Radl"a

רמ"ק
RAMA"K
Ramak
Initials of Rabbi Moshe Kordovero

רמח"ל
Ram'hal
Initials of Rabbi Moshe 'Haim Luzzatto

רע
Ra'
Evil – Bad
See Sitra A'hra

רעוא
Ra'ava
Desire – Will
See Ratson

רעוא דמצחא
Ra'ava Demits'ha
Fourth of the seven Tikunim of the head of Arikh Anpin
From the head of *Partsuf* (configuration) *Arikh Anpin,* seven emanations come out to act and influence on the guidance, called the *Tikunim* of *Arikh Anpin.*

רפ"ח
Rapa'h
288 (numeric value)
See Nitsutsot

רפ"ח נצוצות
Rapa'h Nitsutsot
288 sparks
See Nitsutsot

רצון
Ratson
Will – Desire
All the Kabbalists agree to say that it is not possible to understand, or to have the slightest notion of the Nature of G-od, since our comprehension cannot attain that level. However, we can learn to understand His will, how and why He created the world, in what way He directs it, the provenance of the souls and angels, the purpose of the existence of evil, the reasons for the dualism of reward and punishment, etc.

רצון
Ratson
Name of a *Hekhal* (portal).
Sixth of seven *Hekhalot*, corresponding to *Tiferet*.
The *Hekhalot* are the different levels of ascension of the *Tefilot* (prayers) before reaching the final seventh *Hekhal* (portal); *Kodesh Hakodashim*.

רצון להשפיע
Ratson Lehashpia'
Will to bestow
The will of the Creator is to bestow goodness on His creatures, all the levels of creation were put in place so His kindness could emanate to them, yet in such a way that they would be able to receive it.

רצון לקבל

Ratson Lekabel

Desire to receive

By his nature man is himself a *Keli* (recipient) with a will to receive without limits, and containing a spiritual light; his soul. A guidance based on this desire will permit anything without restriction, and not allow man to merit by his own efforts to get closer to his Creator.

The perfect goal for man is to elevate his bodily desires by sanctifying his ways, and resemble his Creator, by becoming a giver with a will to bestow goodness to all.

רשות

Reshut

Authority – Domain

There is a "second" authority called *Sitra A'hra* or "evil". Even if it is the opposite of everything good, it is important to understand that the origin of "evil" is from an emanation of the superior lights and thus, it does not really have a complete independent authority. It nourishes itself from the lower extremities of the *Kedushah*, and needs permission to act, from above. There is really only one unique authority, and it is the one of the Creator.

רשימו

Reshimu

Imprint – trace

After the *Tsimtsum* (retraction), when His light retracted forming the round space, a trace of it, called *Reshimu,* remained inside. This lower intensity light, allowed a space of existence (*Makom*), for all the created worlds and beings.

The roots of all future existence and events are in the *Reshimu.* Nothing can come into existence, without having its root in this imprint. The combination of the *Kav* and the *Reshimu* is what will give existence to the *Sephirot* with which He governs the worlds.

רשע
Rasha'
Wicked –Sinner
As long as one undertakes the *Tikun* (rectification) of his soul in three reincarnations, he will come back again as needed, to complete his *Tikun*. However, if he maintains his wrong behavior, he will not come back after the third reincarnation.

רש"ש
Rashash
Initials of Rabbi Shalom Sharabi

שבירת הכלים

Shvirat HaKelim

Breaking of the vessels

From the first configuration of *Adam Kadmon* came out different emanations for the construction of the worlds.

From his eyes came out ten *Sephirot* of the aspect of the name of *BaN* (52); they correspond to the feminine aspect - rigor, and are the root of deterioration. When they came out, the higher parts of the first three *Sephirot* of *Keter*, *'Hokhma* and *Binah* received and contained their lights, because they were in the three-column arrangement.

The seven lower *Sephirot* were not in the three pillar arrangement needed for the direction of Kindness, rigor and mercy. Therefore, they could not hold the influx of their lights and broke, their lights stayed in the world of *Atsilut*, their *Kelim* (recipients) fell to the lower worlds.

This caused an important damage called *Shvirat HaKelim* – the breaking of the vessels; this imperfect arrangement is the first origin of the *Sitra A'hra* or "evil".

It is important to understand that all that happens in our world, is similar to what occurred in this fall. If the *Kelim* (recipients) had contained their lights, the *Za"T* would not have broken, and the world would have been in a perfect state from the start.

To sustain the *Kelim* after they broke, 288 sparks of the lights came down as well, because a connection to their original lights was needed to keep them alive. The goal of all the works, deeds and prayers of men in this existence, is to help and participate in the ascent of these sparks to their origin. There are 613 lights in each *Sephira* or *Partsuf* , similarly, there are 613 *Mitsvot*, 613 parts to the soul, and 613 veins and bones to man , this number is not arbitrary, as there are important interrelations and interactions between them.

With the emanation of the lights of *MaH (45)* and *BaN (52)*, He could have done the *Tikun* (rectification) of all the worlds after the *Shvirat HaKelim (breaking of the vessels),* but then, there would not have been a reason for the participation of man in this *Tikun.* It is to give a possibility to man to act and repair the creation, that G-od restrained in a way his outflow of kindness to this world. At the completion of this *Tikun* of unification between the fallen sparks and their *Kelim,* it will be the time of the resurrection of the dead and the arrival of *Moshia'h.*

שבעת מלכין
Shev'at Malkin
Seven kings of Edom – corresponding to Z'aT
See Malkin Kadmain

שבשפה התחתונה
Shebashafa Hata'htona
On the lower lip
Shebashafa Hata'htonah is the fourth of the thirteen *Tikunim* (action) of the *Dikna* (beard) of *Arikh Anpin,* it corresponds to the hair on the lower lip.

שבת
Shabbat
The seventh day, *Shabbat* corresponds to the seventh *Sephira; Malkhut.*

שבתי צבי
Shabbetai Tsevi (1626-1676)
False *Messiah* who was called the "Kabbalistic *Messiah*". He converted to Islam before his death.

This movement caused a severe division in the Jewish community, and mistrust in the teachings of the Kabbalah.

שד-י
Shada-y
One of the names of G-od, represented by the *Sephira Yesod.*

שוא
Shevah
Shevah – Silent vowel
The vowel that represents the *Sephira Gevurah*

שורוק
Shuruk– Vowel U
The vowel that represents the *Sephira Yesod.*

שורש
Shoresh
Root
Every thing and existence has its root in the higher realms.

שטח עליון- מזל נוצר
Shata'h 'Elyon – Mazal Notser
Upper chin
Shata'h 'Elyon – Mazal Notser is the eighth of the thirtheen *Tikunim* (action) of the *Dikna* (beard) of *Arikh Anpin,* it corresponds to the beard on the upper chin.

שטח תחתון
מזל נקה
Sheta'h Ta'hton - Mazal Nake
Lower chin
Sheta'h Ta'hton is the thirteen of the thirtheen *Tikunim* (action) of

the *Dikna* (beard) of *Arikh Anpin;* it corresponds to the beard under the lower chin (*Mazal Nake*).

שיעור
Shi'ur
Measurement
When a *Partsuf* (configuration) is in the stage of *Gadlut* (growth) and has grown to its full size, we say that it has reached its "full measure".

שכולם שוין
Shekulam Shavim
They are all equal
Shekulam Shavim is the eleventh of the thirtheen *Tikunim* (action) of the *Dikna* (beard) of *Arikh Anpin,* it corresponds to they are all equal.

שכינה
Shekhina
Divine presence
One of the names of G-od.
The light of the *Ein Sof* which is revealed by the *Sephira Malkhut* is called *Shekhina*. The goal of all *Tefilot* and *Mitsvot* is to make the *Yi'hud* (union) between *Kudsha Beriah Hu (Z"A)* and the *Shekhina (Malkhut).*

שכינתיה
Shkhinteh
Divine presence
See Shekhina

שכר
Sakhar
Reward

The variable guidance is on the basis of justice, reward and punishment and is dependant on the actions of man. This guidance is by the linear *Sephirot.*

If there was only good in this world, the guidance based on the duality of reward and punishment would not be necessary, but then, men will not have free choice, and no merit for the accomplishment of the will of G-od.

שלם
Shalem
Complete

A *Partsuf* (configuration) is considered complete when it has reached its full potential.

שלמות
Shelemut
Completeness

See Shalem

שמועיא"ל
Shemou'ie"l

Name of one of the three great princes of the Angels.

שמיעה
Shemi'ah
Hearing

From the lights that were invested inside of *Adam Kadmon* emerged numerous worlds in the way of his senses; which are called his branches.

These "branches" are the lights that spread forth from *Adam*

Kadmon, by way of its apertures in the head, four of which are called: Sight, hearing, smell and speech. They spread out from his eyes, ears, nose, and mouth.

From the ears came out lights of the aspect of *SaG.*

See Orot HaOzen

שני נחירים

Shene Ne'hirim

Two nostrils – One of the *Tikunim* of the head of *Arikh Anpin*

From the head of *Partsuf* (configuration) *Arikh Anpin,* seven emanations come out to act and influence on the guidance, called the *Tikunim* of *Arikh Anpin.*

שני תפוחים שנפנו

Shene Tapu'him Shenifenu

Two upper sided of the cheeks

Shene Tapu'him Shenifenu is the seventh of the thirtheen *Tikunim* (action) of the *Dikna* (beard) of *Arikh Anpin,* it corresponds to the two upper sides of the cheeks.

Each one of these *Tikunim* has its particular function or action for the general guidance.

שער

Sha'ar

Gate – Portal

Entrance to a dimension. Gate to enter a knowledge.

שערות

Se'arot

Hairs

There are emanations that come out from the head or face of the *Partsufim* (configurations). They are called hair and beard because they spread out in individual conduits.

שערות הגרון
Se'arot HaGaron
Hair on the throat
Se'arot HaGaron is the tenth of the thirtheen *Tikunim* (action) of the *Dikna* (beard) of *Arikh Anpin;* it corresponds to the hair on the throat.
See Tikun, Partsufim

שערות שבין מזל למזל
Se'arot
sheben Mazal leMazal
Hair between the upper and lower chin
Se'arot sheben Mazal leMazal is the ninth of the thirtheen *Tikunim* (action) of the *Dikna* (beard) of *Arikh Anpin,* it corresponds to the hair between the upper and lower chin.

שערות שבשפה עליונה
Se'arot she baShafa 'Elyonah
Hair on the upper lip
Se'arot she baShafa 'Elyonah is the second of the thirtheen *Tikunim* (action) of the *Dikna* (beard) of *Arikh Anpin,* it corresponds to: The hair on the upper lip.

שפע
Shefa'
Abundance
For the abundance to come down to the world, *Partsuf Zeir Anpin* needs to unite with *Nukvah.* There can be abundance only when the masculine and the feminine are in harmony.
Each day, according to the actions of man, the *Tefilot* (prayers) during the week, *Shabbat* or Holidays, and depending on time, various configurations allow different *Zivugim* (unions), and therefore outflows of abundance of variable intensities.

שקר
Sheker
Falsehood – Lie

The root of the *Sitra A'hra* (negative force) is in the lack, or absence of the *Kedushah*. Its existence was willed by the Creator to give man free will. With falsehood, it almost constantly tries to seduce him, and make him stumble.

See Sitra A'hra

שרעבי
Shar'abi
Rabbi Shalom Shar'abi - The Rashash

Born in Shar'ab, Yemen in 1720, died in Jerusalem in 1777.

After leaving Yemen, he joined the Yeshiva of the Mekubalim "Beth El" in Jerusalem. He is known as the "Master of the Kavanot". His "Siddur HaRashash" is the Siddur (prayer book) used by some Kabbalists in their prayers, and is based on the Kavanot of the Ari Z'al.

תא חזא

Ta 'Haze

Come see (pay attention)

Expression frequently used in the *Zohar.*

תבונה א

Tevunah 1

Partsuf (Reason)

Sephira Malkhut of *Partsuf Imah* is sometimes an independent *Partsuf.*

See Partsufim Israel Saba and Tevunah

תבונה ב

Tevunah 2

Partsuf (Reason) 2

Sephira Malkhut of *Partsuf Tevunah* is sometimes an independent *Partsuf.*

See Partsufim Israel Saba and Tevunah

תגין

Tagin

Crowns on the letters

From the lights that were invested inside of *Adam Kadmon* emerged numerous worlds in the way of his senses; which are called his branches.

The *Sephirot* that came out from the forehead of *Adam Kadmon* for the *Tikun* are of the aspect of the *Tagin* and of the name of *MaH* (45).

תדיר

Tadir

Frequent – Regular

There are regular emanations as the ones of everyday, and exceptions as the emanations of the Holidays and other special occasions.

תולדה

Toladah

Consequence – Result

All the outcomes of the higher emanations are a result of the different unions of the masculine and feminine lights. Each one of these reactions has numerous ramifications, with many details and outcomes and will result in illuminations of different intensities, for the guidance of the worlds.

תורה

Torah

The Kabbalah is the mystical and esoteric explanation of the *Torah*. All the profound secrets explained in the Kabbalah, are alluded in the letters, words and different stories narrated in the *Torah*.

The *Torah* contains four levels of comprehension, of which the highest is the *Sod* (secret). At this level, we understand that our *Tefilot* and the accomplishment of each one of the *Mitsvot,* has a direct influence on the superior worlds and on their guidance.

The *Torah* has 248 positive and 365 negative commandments. Similarly, there are 613 veins and bones to man, 613 parts to the soul, and 613 lights in each *Sephira* or *Partsuf*, this number is not arbitrary, as there are important interrelations and interactions between them.

Through the knowledge of Kabbalah, we can get to a level of true understanding of the will of the Creator, and in a way "decode" the profound secrets of our holy *Torah*.

תחית המתים

T'hiyat ha Metim

Resurrection of the dead

Final goal of the six thousand years.

The *Or* (light) that gives life to the *Keli* (recipient) is comparable to the soul that keeps the body alive. However, when a man dies and his soul separates from his body, the latter will remain with the "*Habela Degarmi*" (הבלא דגרמי), which like the 288 sparks, will allow the conservation of the body from the time the soul has left him, until the resurrection.

At the completion of the *Tikun* (rectification) of unification between the fallen sparks and their *Kelim*, it will be the time of the resurrection of the dead and the arrival of *Moshia'h*.

See Gilgul, 'Ibur

תחת

Ta'hat

Under

What is lower or subordinate.

תחתון

Ta'hton

Inferior – Lower

What is under or subordinate.

תחתונים

Ta'htonim

Lower beings

Separate beings – Angels, men etc.

תיקון
Tikun

Rectification or action

In Hebrew, the word "*Tikun*" has different meanings. It can be understood as reparation or rectification but also as function, relation or action.

There are different types of *Tikunim*:
- *Tikunim* (reparations) that took place in the first emanations to repair the worlds.
- *Tikunim* (rectifications - relations) for the construction and inter-relations of the *Sephirot* and *Partsufim*.
- *Tikunim* (actions - functions) of certain *Partsufim* for the guidance of the world.
- *Tikunim* (rectifications) for the *Neshamot (souls)*.

To repair the *Partsufim* after the *Shvirat HaKelim* (breaking of the vessels), the *Tikun* was the union of the *Sephirot* of *MaH (45)* and *BaN (52)*.

The *Tikunim* for the construction of the *Partsufim* (masculine and feminine) are achieved by way of *Zivug* (union).

For the guidance, the *Tikunim* of the *Partsufim* are the actions, illuminations and inter-relations of the *Sephirot* and *Partsufim*, and their influence on the worlds. These *Tikunim* result in various illuminations of different intensities, depending on time and the actions of man.

For the soul, the *Tikun* is realized by the *Gilgul* (reincarnation), and by the *'Ibur* (attachment). By accomplishing what he did not accomplish of the 613 *Mitsvot*, man makes the necessary *Tikun* of his soul which can now elevate to the higher realms and rejoin its source.

240

By giving man a role in the general *Tikun (Tikun 'Olam),* it is now up to him to restore and make the necessary reparations to the world. However, if man does not act accordingly, the *Tikun* will still be realized, but in the time set by the Creator.

תיקונים
Tikunim
Rectifications or actions
See Tikun

תכלית
Takhlit
Final goal
The goal of all the complex inter-relations and possibilities of guidance have only one purpose: to allow man to merit by his own efforts, to get closer to his Creator and live the *Dvekut* – the adhesion with G-od.
In this way, man will attain perfection and be directly involved in the ultimate goal of the creation, which is the revelation of G-od's sovereignty – *Giluy Ye'hudo.*

תכלת
Tkhelet
Azure
Special color not found at present, which was used on the *Tsitsit* (fringes of the *Talit*).

תלת רישין
Telat Rishin
Three Heads
The three heads of *Arikh Anpin* are the roots of the direction of kindness, rigor and mercy. They emanate from *Arikh Anpin* to *Abah* and *Imah,* and from there, to *Partsuf Z"A.*

241

תמונה

Temunah

Image – Form

Man is as the image of the higher lights, he has 248 limbs and 365 veins. Correspondingly, a *Sephira* or a *Partsuf* comprise of 613 main forces or lights, which afterward divide into many parts. This structure is also similar in the Torah, which has 248 positive and 365 negative commandments.

תניא

Tanya

See Rabbi Shneur Zalman of Liadi

תענוג

Ta'anug

Delight

The utmost delight is to feel closeness to the Creator, by understanding His will and His ways.

תפארת

Tiferet

Sephira (beauty)

Sixth of the *Sephirot*.

Quality: kindness that makes the equilibrium between complete kindness and rigor.

Column: Center – *Ra'hamim* (mercy)

Position: Middle – center

Other *Sephirot* on the same column: *Keter, Yesod, Malkhut*

Partsufim made from this *Sephira*:

One of the *Sephirot* that make the *Partsuf Z"A.*

Corresponding name: YHV-K *י-ה-ו-ה*

Corresponding *Miluy* (spelling) of name: *MaH* (מה) 45

Corresponding vowel: *'Holam*
Physical correspondence: Body
Level of the soul: *Rua'h*
See Sephira, Partsuf

תפילה

Tefilah

Prayer

The order of the *Tefilot* is based on the systems of ascension of
the worlds, as explained in the Kabbalah. At this level, we
understand that our *Tefilot* have a direct influence on the superior
worlds, and on their guidance.

Starting from the first act in the morning of *Netilat Yadayim*
(washing of the hands three times in alternation), until the end of
the *Tefilah*, there is a constant elevation and adhesion of the
worlds of *'Asiah* (action)*, Yetsirah (formation)* and *Beriah
(creation)* to the world of *Atsilut (emanation)*.

This is done by the *Hekhalot* (portals), they are the different levels
of ascension of the *Tefilot* before reaching the *'Olam Atsilut* during
the *'Amidah*. Their principal function is to allow the adhesion and
attachment of these worlds in a precise order.

The goal is to help prepare the different *Partsufim* of *Z"A* and
Nukvah for their *Zivug (union)*.

For the abundance to come down to the world, *Partsuf Zeir
Anpin* needs to unite with *Nukvah*. There can be abundance
only when the masculine and the feminine are in harmony.
Each day, according to the actions of man, the *Tefilot* during
the week, *Shabbat* or Holidays, and depending on time,
various configurations allow different *Zivugim* (unions), and
therefore outflows of abundance of variable intensities.

Each new day, is of a new emanation that governs it. For each
day, there are new *Zivugim* of different aspects of *Z"A* and

Nukvah. A full day is divided in two; day and night, and each half is again divided in two (dawn and day, dusk and night). For each part, there is a *Tefilah,* for the two parts of day: *Sha'hrit* and *Min'ha,* for the two parts of nights: *'Arvit* and *Tikun 'Hatsot.*
Generally, the *Zivugim* are:
Sha'hrit - Ya'acov and *Ra'hel*
Min'ha – Israel and *Leah*
'Arvit – Ya'acov and *Leah* (from the chest up)
Tikun 'Hatsot – Ya'acov and *Leah* (from the chest down)
The *Zivug* of *Israel* and *Ra'hel* is realized during the *Tefilah* of *Musaf* on *Shabbat* and on other special occasions.
When one understands the systems and actions of the *Tefilot,* he realizes the importance of our rituals, because only man, by praying and the accomplishment of the *Mitsvot,* can influence these incredible forces.
See Kavanot, Hekhal (portal), Zivug, Kadish

תפילות
Tefilot
Prayers
See Tefilah

תפילין
Tefilin
Phylacteries
The *Tefilin* represent the lights of the *Mo'hin* (brains) that break out from inside of *Partsuf Z"A* through his forehead.
See Tefilin, Tefilin of Rashi, Tefilin of Rabenu Tam

תפילין דז"א
Tefilin of Z"A
The *Tefilin* on the head correspond to *Partsuf Z"A.*

244

As there are *Mo'hin* from *Abah,* and *Mo'hin* from *Imah,* there are two types of *Tefilin:*

Tefilin of *Imah* – *Rashi*

Tefilin of *Abah* – *Rabenu Tam.*

The difference is in the order of the *Parashiot*:

See Tefilin, Tefilin of Rashi, Tefilin of Rabenu Tam

תפילין דיעקב
Tefilin De Ya'acov
Tefilin of Ya'acov
The *Tefilin* of *Rabenu Tam* on the arm correspond to *Ya'acov.*

תפילין דרבנו תם
Tefilin De Rabenu Tam
Tefilin of Rabenu Tam
The *Mo'hin* from *Abah* make the *Tefilin* of *Rabenu Tam.*
The order of the *Parashiot* is:

1 - 'Hokhma – קדש

2 - Binah - והיה כי יביאך

3 - Gevurot - והיה אם שמוע

4 - 'Hasadim – שמע

See Tefilin, Tefilin of Rashi, Tefilin of Rabenu Tam

תפילין דרחל
Tefilin De Ra'hel
Tefilin of Ra'hel
The *Tefilin* of *Rashi* on the arm correspond to *Ra'hel.*

תפילין דרשי
Tefilin De Rashi
Tefilin of Rashi
The *Mo'hin* from *Imah* make the *Tefilin* of *Rashi.*
The order of the *Parashiot* is:

1 - 'Hokhma – קדש

2 - Binah - והיה כי יביאך

3 - 'Hasadim – שמע

4 - Gevurot - והיה אם שמוע

See Tefilin, Tefilin of Rashi, Tefilin of Rabenu Tam

תקיף

Takif

Hardness

Associated to rigor and *Gevurot.*

תרדמה

Tardema

Sleep – Somnolence

At first *Partsuf Z"A* is in a state of *Tardema* (somnolence), to act it needs to get his *Mo'hin* (brains) from *Partsuf ISOT* or *Partsuf Abah* and *Imah,* and to get to a stage of growth.

תרי"ג

Taryag

613

There are 613 veins and bones to man, similarly, there are 613 *Mitsvot,* 613 parts to the soul, and 613 lights in each *Sephira* or *Partsuf,* this number is not arbitrary, as there are important interrelations and interactions between them.

Index of words

Index

116, 133, 154, 157, 176, 205,
210, 211, 226, 227, 240, 241
Creatures, 31, 32, 35, 63, 87,
92, 97, 100, 108, 133, 154,
157, 160, 176, 226

Da'at, 46, 83, 84, 129, 161, 169,
178
Dikna, 49, 50, 83, 101, 143,
144, 200, 223, 230, 231, 232,
234, 235

Ein Sof, 26, 41, 44, 54, 82, 133,
136, 154, 156, 176, 193, 210,
212, 213, 232
Emanation, 56
Emanations, 66, 145
Encircling lights, 47, 87
Evil, 13, 28, 33, 56, 153, 173,
176, 181, 188, 211, 216, 227,
229

Forces, 13, 34, 35, 43, 45, 50,
53, 69, 82, 89, 99, 108, 114,
115, 124, 137, 139, 153, 174,
193, 202, 203, 211, 216, 243

Gadlut, 71, 72, 78, 141, 209,
232
G"aR, 69, 128, 162
Gestation, 72, 81, 87, 94, 118,
132, 169, 189, 215
Gevurah, 55, 64, 69, 70, 82, 86,
87, 98, 99, 102, 109, 111,
137, 157, 160, 161, 168, 178,
203, 231, 267
Gevurot, 51, 71, 83, 89, 109,
149, 152, 209, 245, 246
Gilgul, 76, 130, 153, 189, 240
G-od, 36, 45, 54, 55, 74, 80,
114, 116, 155, 231, 241
Growth, 71, 72, 81, 88, 93, 100,
102, 109, 118, 123, 132, 141,
169, 208, 209, 232, 246

Guidance, 13, 29, 30, 31, 32,
34, 35, 36, 48, 49, 50, 51, 62,
63, 69, 74, 76, 80, 82, 89, 97,
99, 100, 108, 114, 116, 121,
124, 128, 134, 137, 139, 153,
160, 162, 168, 180, 181, 188,
200, 201, 203, 205, 211, 222,
223, 224, 227, 233, 234, 238,
240, 241, 243
Guided, 13, 34, 89, 153, 154,
202, 211
Guides, 66, 196
Gulgolta, 77, 78

'Hasadim, 71, 83, 89, 93, 109,
149, 154, 164, 196, 245

HBD, 47, 102, 127, 168
Hekhal, 45, 87, 99, 124, 130,
160, 195, 213, 226
Hekhalot, 45, 87, 99, 124, 130,
149, 160, 195, 213, 226

'Hesed, 45, 65, 69, 82, 87, 98,
99, 107, 108, 109, 111, 137,
139, 157, 167, 168, 174, 178,
180, 192, 203, 224, 267

HGT, 47, 76, 102, 127, 168,
209, 215
Hokhma, 28, 41, 46, 49, 55, 56,
69, 107, 109, 111, 114, 125,
128, 129, 131, 140, 143, 144,
161, 162, 167, 178, 203, 206,
219, 220, 229, 245

'Ibur, 76, 78, 130, 153, 189,
240

Imah, 41, 45, 46, 47, 55, 56, 57,
58, 64, 72, 77, 81, 104, 120,
123, 140, 141, 164, 166, 171,
186, 196, 203, 208, 209, 215,
220, 237, 241, 244, 245, 246

Mo'hin, 46, 47, 71, 72, 77, 78,
  81, 83, 123, 133, 140, 141,
  142, 154, 160, 209, 244, 245

Nekudim, 170, 187
Nekudot, 51, 112, 170
Neshama, 64, 76, 104, 106,
  117, 121, 164, 166, 170, 171,
  194, 220
Neshamot, 57, 78, 79, 172, 195,
  207, 240
NHY, 47, 55, 72, 76, 81, 127,
  141, 142, 159, 168, 169, 208,
  209, 215
Nitsutsot, 28, 162, 164, 225,
  226
Nukvah, 56, 57, 58, 59, 71, 80,
  83, 87, 94, 95, 97, 109, 120,
  123, 127, 129, 133, 136, 145,
  146, 151, 154, 156, 160, 161,
  169, 175, 186, 196, 199, 203,
  209, 210, 220, 223, 235, 243

Or, 46, 47, 85, 87, 111, 122,
  126, 156, 178, 201, 214, 239
Or Makif, 47, 87, 111, 156
Orot, 48, 49, 50, 82, 112, 190,
  224, 233

Partsuf, 30, 31, 41, 44, 47, 53,
  55, 58, 66, 87, 94, 95, 98,
  100, 118, 119, 120, 122, 123,
  126, 129, 132, 141, 142, 144,
  152, 154, 160, 164, 168, 169,
  192, 195, 196, 198, 199, 203,
  205, 209, 210, 214, 223, 237
Partsufim, 18, 41, 45, 51, 52,
  53, 55, 56, 57, 58, 62, 64, 66,
  69, 70, 82, 83, 86, 87, 92, 94,
  97, 99, 100, 104, 107, 108,
  109, 110, 115, 117, 118, 119,
  120, 122, 123, 127, 129, 131,
  132, 137, 139, 145, 146, 149,
  151, 152, 156, 160, 164, 166,
  167, 168, 169, 171, 178, 181,

  184, 186, 187, 189, 196, 198,
  199, 200, 201, 202, 203, 205,
  216, 220, 223, 237, 240, 242,
  243
Pillars, 53
Punishment, 13, 33, 35, 56, 89,
  188, 211, 233

Ra'hel, 123, 129, 208, 223, 245
Ratson, 87, 92, 198, 226, 227,
  267
Receive, 13, 23, 35, 36, 63, 92,
  108, 133, 141, 154, 157, 176,
  210, 211, 226, 227
Reshimu, 26, 44, 47, 106, 155,
  180, 213, 222, 227
Resurrection, 28, 85, 153, 162,
  185, 229, 239
Returning lights, 46
Reward, 13, 33, 35, 56, 89, 188,
  211, 233
Rigor, 28, 46, 48, 49, 52, 55,
  58, 61, 63, 64, 69, 70, 77, 82,
  86, 97, 99, 108, 126, 129,
  134, 137, 139, 140, 162, 168,
  176, 178, 180, 181, 187, 188,
  200, 201, 203, 210, 223, 224,
  229, 241, 242, 246
Rigors, 51, 64, 71, 83, 89, 109,
  149, 152, 154, 178, 209, 218
Rigors, 25, 69, 70, 71, 82, 137,
  168, 178
Rua'h, 70, 76, 86, 104, 109,
  117, 119, 164, 166, 167, 171,
  216, 220, 222, 242

SaG, 48, 51, 64, 82, 112, 173,
  183, 184, 185, 193, 194, 199,
  224
Secrets, 136, 211
Sepher Hayetsira, 43, 122, 207
Sephira, 41, 43, 45, 47, 51, 53,
  54, 55, 62, 64, 68, 69, 70, 82,
  83, 85, 86, 102, 103, 106,
  107, 109, 114, 115, 119, 126,

Bibliography

From the Ram'hal

כללות האילן הקדוש
פתחי חכמה ודעת
קלח פתחי חכמה
כללים ראשונים
אדיר במרום

From the Ari Z'al

כתבי האריי
עץ חיים
שער רוח הקודש
שער הגלגולים

ספר הזהר
The Zohar
Rabbi Shim'on Bar Yo'hai

The Kabbalah of the Ari Z'al, according to the Ramhal
Rabbi Raphael Afilalo, Kabbalah Editions

Kabbalah Dictionary
Rabbi Raphael Afilalo, Kabbalah Editions

דרך חכמת האמת לרמחל
Rav Mordekhai Chriqui, Editions Ramhal, Jerusalem

האילן הקדוש לרמחל
Rav Shalom Oulman (Jerusalem)

Tables

Different levels of the souls

Soul / World	'Asiah	Yetsirah	Beriah	Atsilut	Atsilut
Nefesh	Nukvah	Nukvah	Nukvah	Nukvah	Nukvah
Nefesh	Zeir	Zeir	Zeir	Zeir	Zeir
Nefesh	Imah	Imah	Imah	Imah	Imah
Nefesh	Abah	Abah	Abah	Abah	Abah
Nefesh	Arikh	Arikh	Arikh	Arikh	Arikh
Rua'h	Nukvah	Nukvah	Nukvah	Nukvah	Nukvah
Rua'h	Zeir	Zeir	Zeir	Zeir	Zeir
Rua'h	Imah	Imah	Imah	Imah	Imah
Rua'h	Abah	Abah	Abah	Abah	Abah
Rua'h	Arikh	Arikh	Arikh	Arikh	Arikh
Neshama	Nukvah	Nukvah	Nukvah	Nukvah	Nukvah
Neshama	Zeir	Zeir	Zeir	Zeir	Zeir
Neshama	Imah	Imah	Imah	Imah	Imah
Neshama	Abah	Abah	Abah	Abah	Abah
Neshama	Arikh	Arikh	Arikh	Arikh	Arikh
'Hayah	Nukvah	Nukvah	Nukvah	Nukvah	Nukvah
'Hayah	Zeir	Zeir	Zeir	Zeir	Zeir
'Hayah	Imah	Imah	Imah	Imah	Imah
'Hayah	Abah	Abah	Abah	Abah	Abah
'Hayah	Arikh	Arikh	Arikh	Arikh	Arikh
Ye'hidah	Nukvah	Nukvah	Nukvah	Nukvah	Nukvah
Ye'hidah	Zeir	Zeir	Zeir	Zeir	Zeir
Ye'hidah	Imah	Imah	Imah	Imah	Imah
Ye'hidah	Abah	Abah	Abah	Abah	Abah
Ye'hidah	Arikh	Arikh	Arikh	Arikh	Arikh

Hekhalot (portals)

	Hekhal / Portal	Corresponding to
First	לבנת הספיר (*Livnat Hasapir*)	*Yesod* and *Malkhut*
Second	עצם השמים (*Etsem Hashamayim*)	*Hod*
Third	נוגה (*Nogah*)	*Netsa'h*
Fourth	זכות (*Zekhut*)	*Gevurah*
Fifth	אהבה (*Ahavah*)	*'Hesed*
Sixth	רצון (*Ratson*)	*Tiferet*
Seventh	קדש קדשים (*Kodesh Kodashim*)	*Keter, 'Hokhma, Binah*

Sephirot

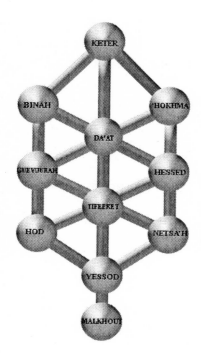

Rigor	Mercy	Kindness
	Keter *Crown*	
Binah *Understanding*		**'Hokhma** *Wisdom*
	Da'at Knowledge	
Gevurah *Rigor*		**'Hesed** *Bounty*
	Tiferet *Beauty*	
Hod *Splendor*		**Netsa'h** *Glory*
	Yesod *Foundation*	
	Malkhut *Kingship*	

265

Vowels

Sephira	Vowel
Keter	Kamatz
'Hokhma	Pata'h
Binah	Tsere
'Hesed	Segol
Gevurah	Shevah
Tiferet	'Holam
Netsa'h	'Hirik
Hod	Kubutz
Yesod	Shuruk
Malkhut	No vowel

The seven main planets correspond to seven Sephirot

Sephira	Planet	
'Hesed	Moon	לבנה
Gevurah	Mars	מאדים
Tiferet	Sun	חמה
Netsa'h	Venus	נוגה
Hod	Mercury	כוכב
Yesod	Saturn	שבתאי
Malkhut	Jupiter	צדק

266

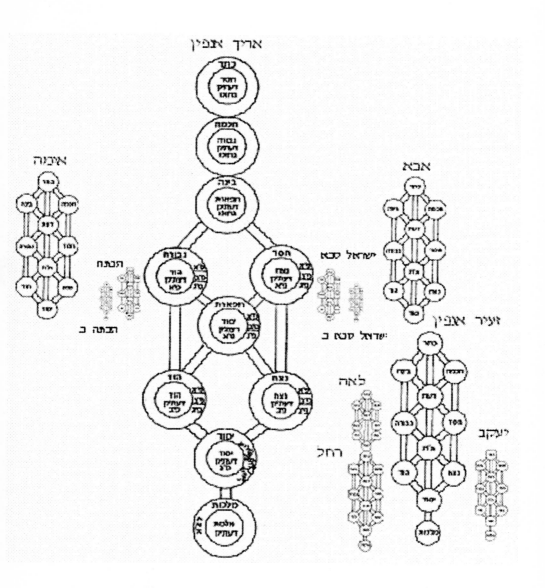

267

POSITION OF THE SEPHIROT

Sephira	Column	Position	Letter
Keter	Crown	Mercy	Center	א
'Hokhma	Wisdom	Kindness	Right	ה
Binah	Understanding	Rigor	Left	ע
Da'at	Knowledge	Mercy	Center	
'Hesed	Bounty	Kindness	Right	ב
Gevurah	Rigor	Rigor	Left	ג
Tiferet	Beauty	Mercy	Center	ד
Netsa'h	Glory	Kindness	Right	כ
Hod	Splendor	Rigor	Left	פ
Yesod	Foundation	Mercy	Center	ר
Malkhut	Kingship	Mercy	Center	ת

SEPHIRA – SOUL – PARTSUF – NAME

Sephira	Level of the soul	Partsuf	Tetragamon	
Keter	Ye'hidah	'Atik Yomin Arikh Anpin	**·**	Extremity of Yud
'Hokhma	Hayah	Abah Israel Saba	**·**	Yud
Binah	Neshamah	Imah Tevunah	ה	First HeY
'Hesed	Rua'h	Zeir Anpin	ו	Vav
Gevurah	Rua'h	Zeir Anpin	ו	Vav
Tiferet	Rua'h	Zeir Anpin	ו	Vav
Netsa'h	Rua'h	Zeir Anpin	ו	Vav
Hod	Rua'h	Zeir Anpin	ו	Vav
Yesod	Rua'h	Zeir Anpin	ו	Vav
Malkhut	Nefesh	Nukvah	ה	Second HeY

SEPHIRA – NAME – MILUY – TaNTA

Sephira	Name		Miluy		TaNTA	
Keter	אהי-ה	AHY-H	שע	A"V	72	Ta'amim	Cantillations
'Hokhma	י-ה	YH	שע	'A"V	72	Ta'amim	Cantillations
Binah	י-ה-ו-ה (with the vowels of Elohi-m)	YHV-H	סג	SaG	63	Nekudim	Vowels
Da'at	אהו-ה	AHV-H					
'Hesed	אל	EL	מה	MaH	45	Tagin	Crowns
Gevurah	אלהי-ם	Elohi-m	מה	MaH	45	Tagin	Crowns
Tiferet	י-ה-ו-ה	YHV-H	מה	MaH	45	Tagin	Crowns
Netsa'h	יהו-ה-י צבאות	YKVK Tsebaot	מה	MaH	45	Tagin	Crowns
Hod	אלהי-ם צבאות	Elohi-m Tsebaot	מה	MaH	45	Tagin	Crowns
Yesod	שד-י	Shada-y	מה	MaH	45	Tagin	Crowns
Malkhut	אדנ-י	Adona-y	בן	BaN	52	Autiot	Letters

PARTICULARITY OF THE SEPHIROT

Sephira	Quality
Keter	Complete kindness to all, even to the not deserving
'Hokhma	Kindness to all, even to the not deserving (but less than Keter, and not always)
Binah	Kindness to all, even to the less deserving (but from her, the rigors start)
Da'at	Guidance that makes the equilibrium between 'Hokhmah and Binah
'Hesed	Complete kindness to who is deserving
Gevurah	Full rigor to who is deserving
Tiferet	Kindness that makes the equilibrium between complete kindness and rigor
Netsa'h	Diminished kindness to who is deserving
Hod	Diminished rigor to who is deserving.
Yesod	Guidance that makes the equilibrium between Sephira Netsa'h and Hod
Malkhut	Guidance that translates all the superior emanations into one that is reflected to the creation Link or connection between all the superior Sephirot and man

SEPHIRA – BODY – DAY – METAL - DIRECTION

Sephira	Physical correspondence	Face	Day	Metal	Direction
Keter	Head	Head			
'Hokhma	Right brain	Right brain			
Binah	Left brain	Left brain			
'Hesed	Right arm	Right eye	Sunday	Silver	South
Gevurah	Left arm	Right ear	Monday	Gold	North
Tiferet	Body	Right nostril	Tuesday	Copper	East
Netsa'h	Right leg	Left eye	Wednesday	Tin	Above
Hod	Left leg	Left ear	Thursday	Lead	Lower
Yesod	Masculine organ	Left nostril	Friday	Silver	West
Malkhut	Crown on the masculine organ	Mouth	Shabbat	Iron	Center

GEMATRIA

Letters		Ragil	Katan:	HaKadmi	HaKlali	Kolel	HaPerati	Miluy
		Regular number of the letters	Tens and hundreds are reduced to one digit.	Each letter has its Ragil value plus the total of all the ones preceding it.	The Ragil value of the word squared	The Ragil value of the word + the numbers of letters, or + 1 for the word.	Each letter is squared	The sum of the spelling of each letter
From	To							
א	ט	1 - 9	1 - 9	1 - 45				
י	צ	10 - 90	1 - 9	55 – 495				
ק	ת	100 - 400	1 - 4	595 – 1495				
ך	ץ	500 - 900	5 - 9	1995 – 4995				

לעלוי נשמת

Abraham David Hanania Afilalo bar Mira ז'ל
Rav Abraham Chocron ז'ל
Salomon Afilalo ז'ל
Mira Afilalo ז'ל
Gracia Chocron ז'ל

לעלוי נשמת

Rav Yeich Revah ז'ל
Joseph Revah ז'ל
Yacot Revah ז'ל
Sylvie Revah ז'ל
Israel Kakone ז'ל
Simi Kakone ז'ל
Mardoche Kakone ז'ל
Salomon Kakone ז'ל

From Mr. Daniel Revah

לעלוי נשמת

Deborah Elbaz Bat Aziza ז'ל
La'hziz Gozlan ז'ל
Its'hak Chokron ז'ל
Moshe Afilalo ז'ל
Meyer Ohayon ז'ל
Meir Mergui ז'ל
Its'hak Mergui ז'ל
David Ohnona ז'ל
Richard Gabbay ז'ל
Eliran Elbaz ben Yardena ז'ל
David Haim Benyamin Knafo ז'ל

Printed in the United States
42766LVS00003B/103-111